BOOKSHELF
Design

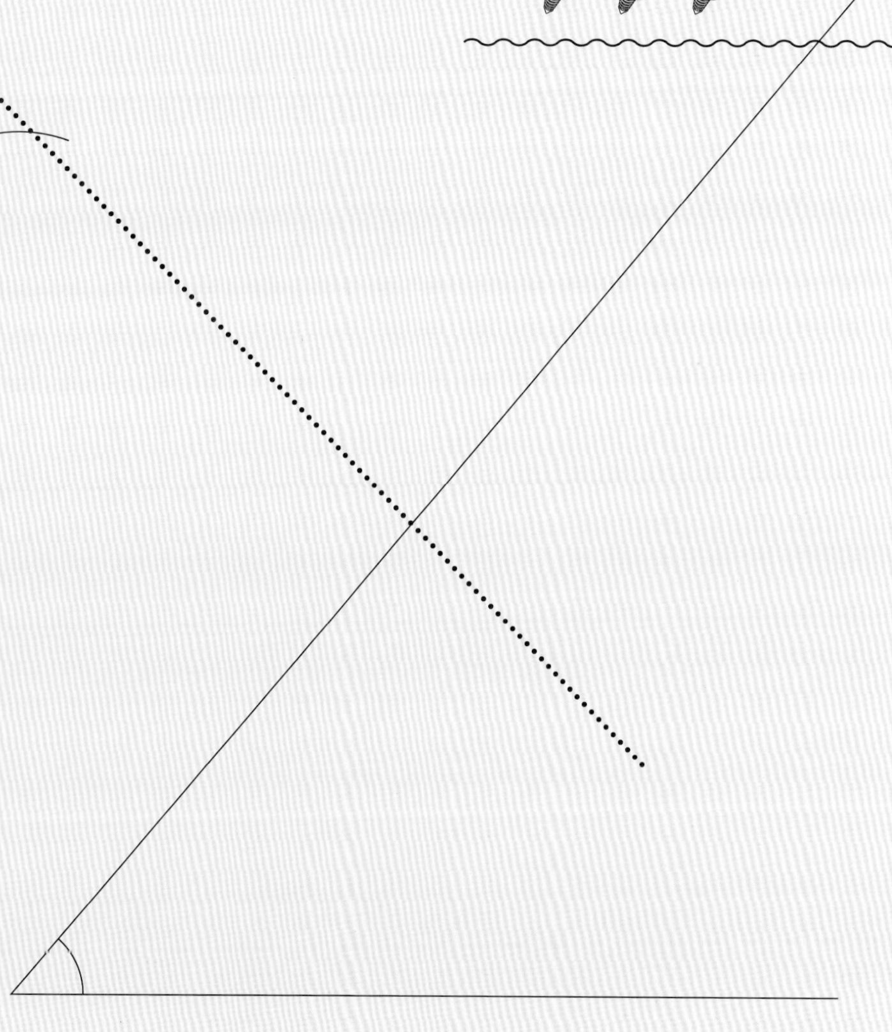

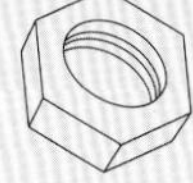

Bookshelf Design

EDITED & PUBLISHED BY SendPoints Publishing Co., Ltd.
PUBLISHER: Lin Gengli
PUBLISHING DIRECTOR: Lin Shijian
EDITORIAL DIRECTOR: Sundae Li
EXECUTIVE EDITOR: Li Weiji, Zhong Yuanwen, Ma Xiaojian
ART DIRECTOR: He Wanling
EXECUTIVE ART EDITOR: Peng Lingbo
PROOFREADING: Sundae Li, Heart Fensch

ADDRESS: Room 15A Block 9 Tsui Chuk Garden, Wong Tai Sin, Kowloon, Hong Kong
TEL: +852-35832323 / **FAX:** +852-35832448
EMAIL: info@sendpoints.cn

DISTRIBUTED BY Guangzhou SendPoints Book Co., Ltd.
SALES MANAGER: Zhang Juan (China), Sissi (International)
GUANGZHOU: +86-20-89095121
BEIJING: +86-10-84139071
SHANGHAI: +86-21-63523469
EMAIL: overseas01@sendpoints.cn
WEBSITE: www.SendPoints.cn

ISBN 978-988-12944-4-9

Printed and bound in China

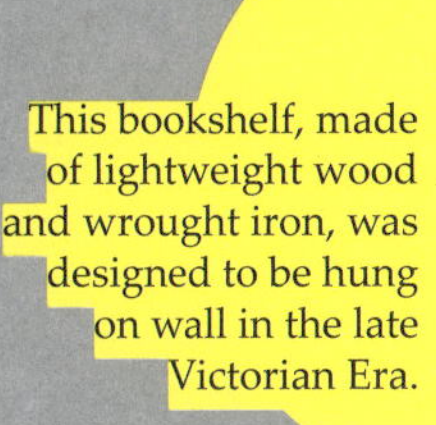

This bookshelf, made of lightweight wood and wrought iron, was designed to be hung on wall in the late Victorian Era.

This Danner revolving bookcase was designed in the late Victorian Era, with primary purpose in keeping reference books. In addition to the revolving fact, castors could be assembled to make it movable in the library or study.

s,
ry.
ooks,
te
ooks

Late 19th century

Hanging/sliding bookcase appeared in the British Museum Library in the late 19th century, as an expansion to accommodate the increasing number of books.

At the beginning of the 20th century

The Bookmobile designed for hospital patients in 1928—Los Angeles Library.

The 21st century

Stylish modern bookshelf.

* A design featured on P141 of this book

19th C.

20th C.

21th C.

k spine

ustration, the books were stored
g outwards.

From this 15th century manuscript we could see a scholar (c.347-420) using a lectern with slots for scrolls.

Middle Ages

Large volume of books was kept in monasteries. They were locked in chests that were usually lifted up from ground for easier transportation and protection from dampness.

There were standing lectern and lectern with a bench to sit on.

At the end of the 12th century

Some books in a monastery were kept in this recess in the wall of a cloister.

12th C.

13th C.

14th C.

Outward fore

The ring fixed on the c
chaining the book to th
books were always she
fore-edge facing outwa

The big wheel shelf invented by Agostino Ramelli in 1588.

A scholar in the 15th century, Isotta Nogarola, was using a revolving lectern.

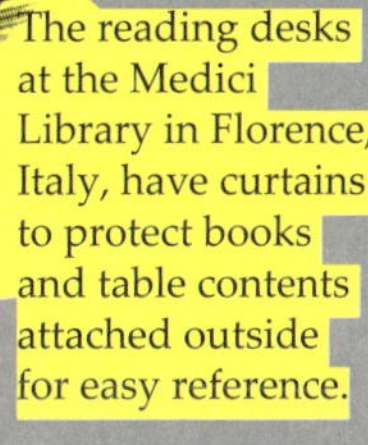

The reading desks at the Medici Library in Florence, Italy, have curtains to protect books and table contents attached outside for easy reference.

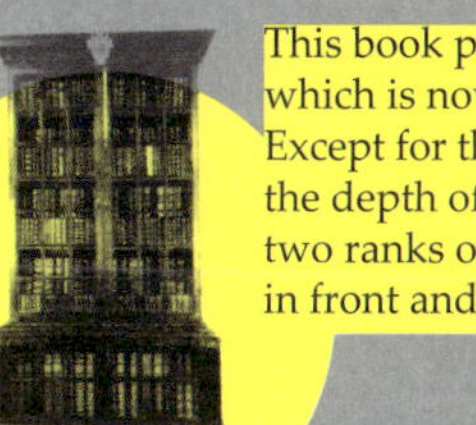

This book press belonged to Sar
which is now preserved in the P
Except for the shelf that stores t
the depth of every shelf could a
two ranks of books, in which th
in front and the taller ones at ba

An avid reader in the 15th century was reading with a pair of glasses. We could observe the way the books were arranged on the shelves and in the cabinet.

Early 15th century

These reading desks, located in the Old Library at Lincoln Cathedral in early 15th century, had shelves fitted both in the upper and lower parts.

Late 16th century

In the late 16th century, the books in the library of Peterhouse were no longer chained to the shelves. This means that the seats could be removed and more room was made for books.

Late 17th century

Stall system and wall syst
were both shown in this depiction of 1675.

15th C.

16th C.

17th C.

18th C.

-edge

ver was for
e shelf. The
ved with the
rds.

Book spine came into sight

In the 16th century book spine with the author's name and book title appeared, though shelving books with outward spine was not yet the general practice.

Outwa

In this 18th
with their s

The multifunctional

The stylish & The intriguing

PREFACE

Functional Design

By designer Jiyoung Seo

In a world overwhelmed by information where a flash drive stores the knowledge on a million books, the idea of a bookshelf seems a little too romantic. A bookshelf carries the one thing a memory card failed to save—memory. Designer bookshelves embody the creative professional's pursuit of aesthetics and functionality.

When a designer controls a hundred percent the making of a product, it becomes more or less useful to the user. When a designer gives the control of a space to the user, a product can be redefined in so many different ways based on the user's needs and imaginations. The product can then become an object with a personal touch to the user.

For example, here are two stools. One is a typical standard stool. The other one was designed to have a hole in the middle. This hole makes a world of difference. It opens up the possibilities of using the stool in a wide variety of ways. The design is then connected with the user's specific character and needs. This is possible when a designer interact with the user and applies connected thinking with a user. For the connected thinking, observation is vital.

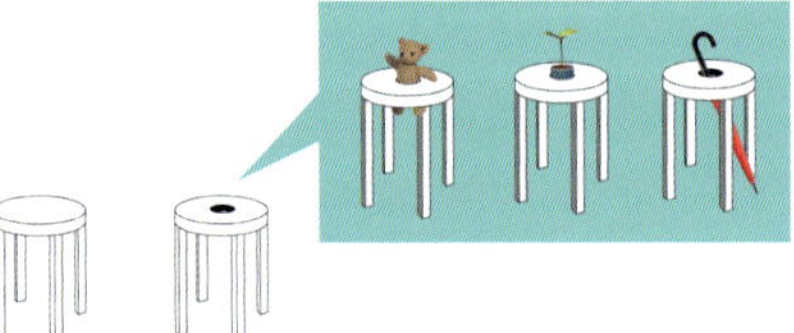

When I start to design a product, I tend to focus on user experience and customer behaviors which I believe is crucial to my design. I would look at the general design process first and then concentrate on the environment and people's behavior which is interconnected with the environment. This observation allows a designer to recognize what people are looking for in a product. Soulful design

comes from a design based on connected thinking with user.

There are basic bookshelves and those with a unique design featuring different materials, structures, shapes and so on. The structure can give an intriguing character to a bookshelf. The projects presented on this inspiring book include bookshelf sofas, lamps, sculptures, and even paintings, to name but a few. These shelves are interactive with the user and in many ways say something about the character of the user.

Material is also one vital aspect that presents a style to a certain design. The same applies to the design a bookshelf. In Bookshelf design creation, there are numerous creative products made out of wood, plastic and metal. The possibility in the choice of materials is wide open. It can be fabric, rubber, paper or anything you can think of. Different texture brings about varying styles and touch in product design. The sense of touch is the most sensitive one among the five senses. It is the first sense that we experience at birth, and the last of the senses that are lost upon death.

Thus, the bank of textural intelligence we accumulate through everyday experience becomes an important means of communication; and the direct link between a product's function and its emotive qualities becomes apparent. With some of my design, I explore this approach by keeping in mind not to focus on the product itself or its appearance only, but also highlight the importance of its texture.

CONTENTS

The multifunctional

The stylish & The intriguing

The multifunctional

BOOK LAMP

» Groupa Design Studio

» Israel

This is a striking and minimalistic hanging lamp for reading. To call this lamp a book shelf might sound like a bit of a stretch, but it is definitely eye-catching and refreshing. The concept makes it easy to imagine a relaxing night spent reading a book under a yellowish light in a warm and comfy room.

SHELVING CHAIR

» Jun Murakoshi
» Japan

Stacking Chair is a very practical, space-saving design. But once the chairs are stacked, they inevitably lose their functional and aesthetic appeal. In contrast, this product is expected to most often be utilized as a modular shelving unit, however it can also become a chair when needed. This chair is made of beech timber, birch plywood, MDF laminated paper, honeycomb panel and felt. A honeycomb panel was used inside each board to make it much lighter than solid timber or plywood with less material. The felt on the back was selected to make it easier to stack up and more comfortable to sit on.

Photo ©Takafumi Yamada, Noritake

ANYTHING CAN BE INSERTED ANYWHERE.

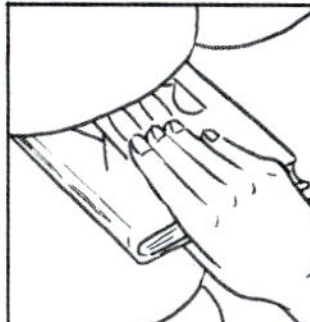

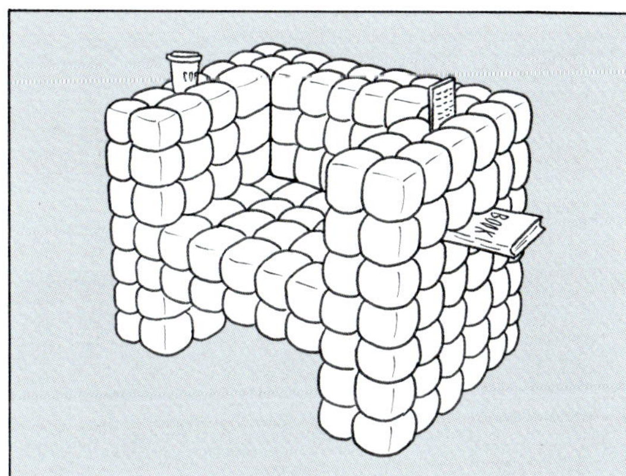

LOST IN SOFA

› Daisuke Motogi
› Japan

Things often get lost under the sofa. Everyone has found things like coins or even a TV remote underneath the sofa cushions. If one gets lucky they might even find a small treasure that was once left there. Because of that, if people want to store the things they treasure, this furniture can help.

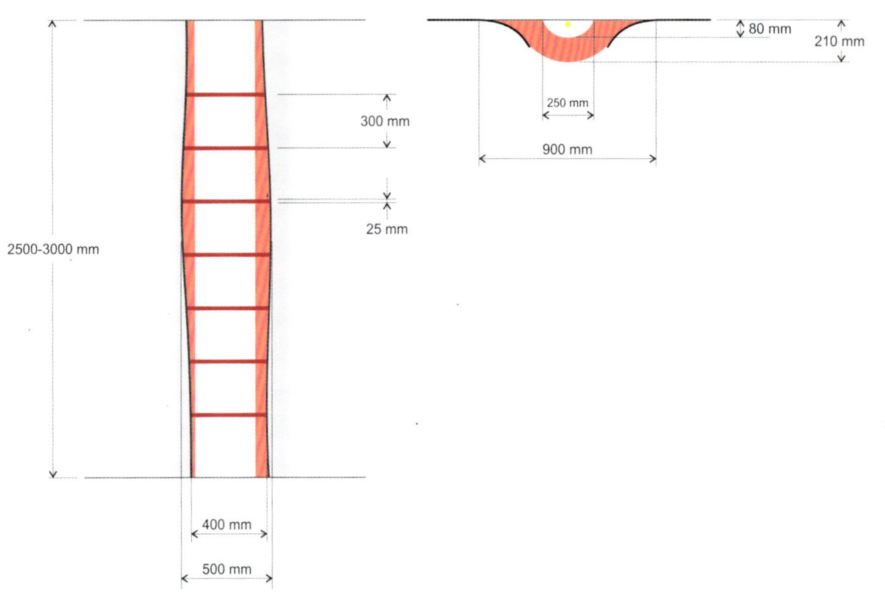
80 mm
210 mm
250 mm
900 mm
300 mm
25 mm
2500-3000 mm
400 mm
500 mm

CUTSHELVES

» Tembolat Gugkaev
» Russia

This is a bookshelf which is built into the wall and designed with a sleek shape. Coupled with the backlighting, it offers better visibility during the night.

CAMEL LIGHT

» Groupa Design Studio
» Israel

An innovative bookshelf inspired by the desert and its famous inhabitant with a hump: the camel. Camels are exceptionally well-suited for carrying loads in deserts, which gave the designers the idea of making a camel-shaped bookshelf that also functions as a lamp. The bookshelf is 100% Israeli design, made out of birch plywood and metal bending.

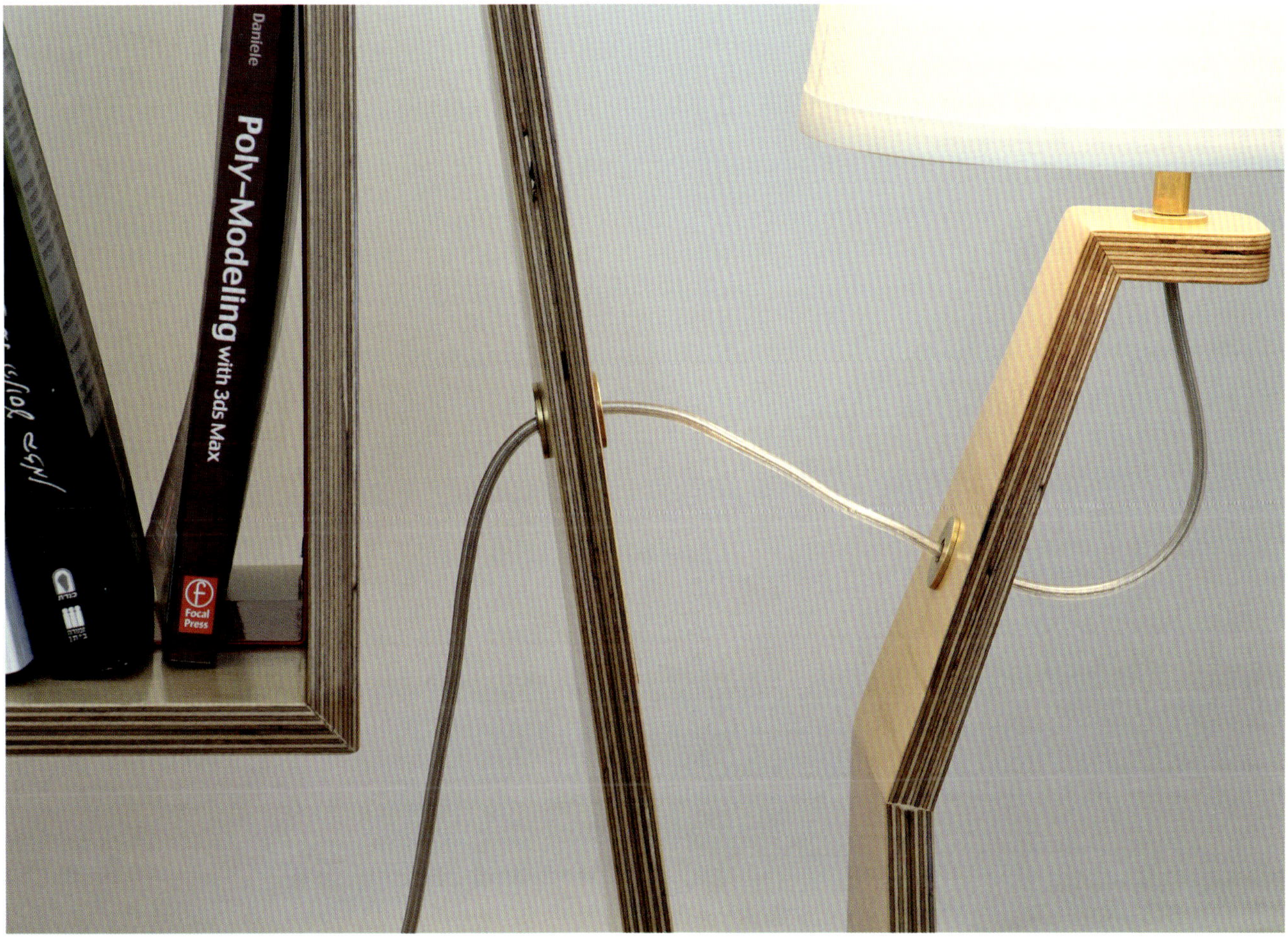

ATLAS OF ANATOMY
Working with Wood

L'ILLÉTRÉE

» Chloé HUEBER
» France

When an object is put away, it can be hidden or even forgotten. L'Illétrée explores the concepts of "hidden things" and "revealed things" by unveiling a part of the objects that have been put away. The book edge is shown while its spine is hidden, in order to visually both soften and lighten the bookshelf surroundings. A poetic atmosphere emanates from the bookshelf with the LED lamps lighting up the books. The light halo encourages the user to read and contemplate.

WHA CABINET

› Tembolat Gugkaev
› Russia

Wha Cabinet is an interesting and multi-functional bookshelf, which is a combination of closet, cabinet and lamp. During the day, it is a cabinet and works as a lamp at night. Dressed in a curvy look with color backlit shelves, this interesting cabinet brings urbane sophistication and style. With its simple, neat, elegant and multipurpose features, it is a perfect contemporary design.

EASY READER

» Nils Holger Moormann
» Germany

With Easy Reader, you can read, sit and even load objects which need to be moved. It clearly brings together fun and reading. The designer hopes that readers will find peace of mind through reading while sitting and relaxing mentally on Easy Reader.

Photo ©JÄGERD JAGER

THE BIBLIOCHAISE

» Giovanni Gennari, Alisée Matta
» Italy

Geometry can be magical every time you draw a cube or a square, something wonderful can happen. To find space to sit and to keep a number of books in a tiny flat is not easy. Problems inspire creativity. To solve this problem, the designers made a creative bookshelf by drawing a cube as a sofa with slots all around it to put the books in.

Photo ©Fishtnk Inc

BOOKSEAT

» Fishtnk Design Factory
» Canada

The Bookseat is a simple multifunctional bookcase that playfully curves and becomes a seat. It represents a creative design responding to the advent of multifunctional spaces in today's urban life. The piece is locally sourced and hand-crafted, and will be available with a felt cushion in customizable colors and a limited edition leather cushion. The current production of the Bookseat is limited to 100 pieces, which are uniquely numbered and tagged.

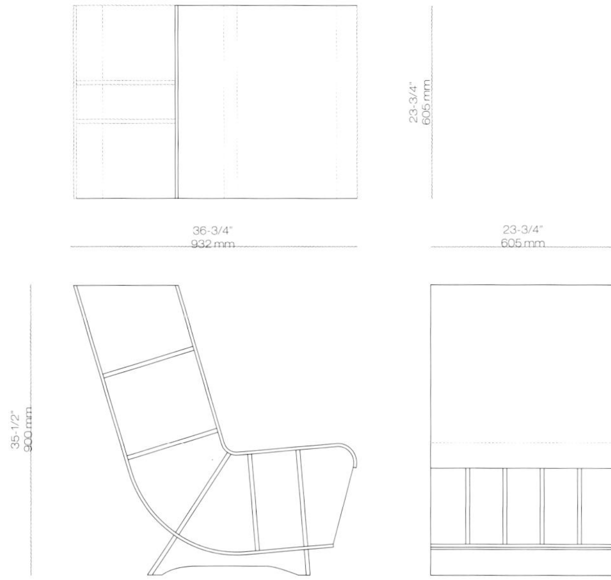

TO OBSERVE

Being an architect focusing on human interaction with habitable space, I have become an observer of how we occupy the spaces we live in. Modern urban living requires efficient space planning and multipurpose features to make the best of our everyday life.

THE STORY BEHIND

I usually start with something tangible, something that works and could be improved. This time it happened to be a bookshelf. Bookcases are usually associated with heavy, static pieces of furniture that are usually pushed to the sides of the room. The spark of the idea was how to bring the books into the middle of the space and celebrate their presence.

I was reading an essay on architecture of Le Corbusier and his definition of space. The essay brought the inefficiencies and waste of space to my attention, and this is his quote: "We cannot revise the plans for contemporary houses effectively unless we take a new look at the furniture question…Furniture, apart from chairs and tables consists almost entirely of storage space. And existing storage units generally have the wrong dimensions and are practically unusable. I condemn such waste of space." - Le Corbusier, 1930.

In an interesting way these two ideas came together and filled each other's gaps to incarnate the Bookseat.

SHELFLIFE RANGE

» Charles Trevelyan
» UK

The genesis of this project was an observation made while watching people browse a bookshelf. People would frequently find a book of interest, and then try to flick through the pages, often while carrying several books or other items. Incorporating a chair and small side table into the bookshelf enables a person to more easily browse through books as they find them or even stay a while to read.

The form and structure of the piece were derived entirely from the premise of integrating a chair into a bookshelf in a way that the chair blends into the shelves. The angles of the shelves were an extension of the angles in the chair. They also served both to camouflage the extra functionality of the piece, and to add a level of visual intrigue to an often understated furniture type.

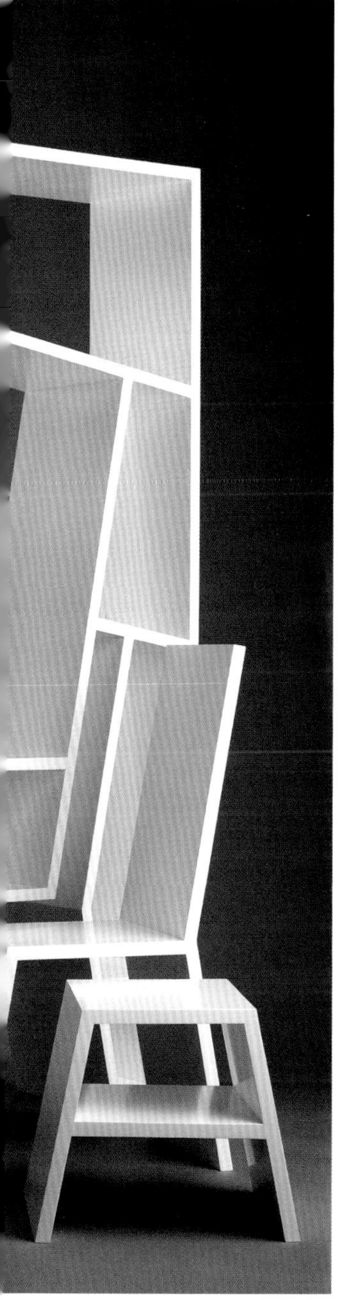

Photo ©George Ong, Rachel Smith & Charles Trevelyan

FAMILY SHELF PORTRAITS

› Darragh Casey
› UK

Shelf Portraits and See Saw Shelf are from "Shelving the Body" series. In Shelf Portraits Darragh Casey explored the shelf's role as an item to display objects that are sentimental or memorable in our lives. As he was shelving people, he decided to display people who are important to him. So the designer created Family Shelf Portraits that shelved three generations of his family alongside objects that are important to them.

Each "Shelf Portrait" was designed to reflect the personality of the individuals on the shelves. For grandmother, traditional, horizontal lines like an old Irish Dresser have been used. She chose objects that represented her life and generation and displayed them in a traditional way. The designer's and his brothers' shelf portraits were a contrast to this, reflecting the younger generation, showing how they are connected as brothers. So each brother was displayed with his own objects around – even the family dog was displayed! The concept of parents' shelf portrait reveals how they rely on each other. If one of them moves, the other one is not supported. It represents their relationship as well as their individual personalities.

ROCKING SHELF

› Darragh Casey
› UK

Rocking Shelf is a storage device that stimulates a sense of childlike play for the user. The shelf was designed to allow the user to rock from side to side while they read or interact with the shelved objects. It comprises a single bent ply seat that "shelves" the figure rather than offer them a comfortable seat.

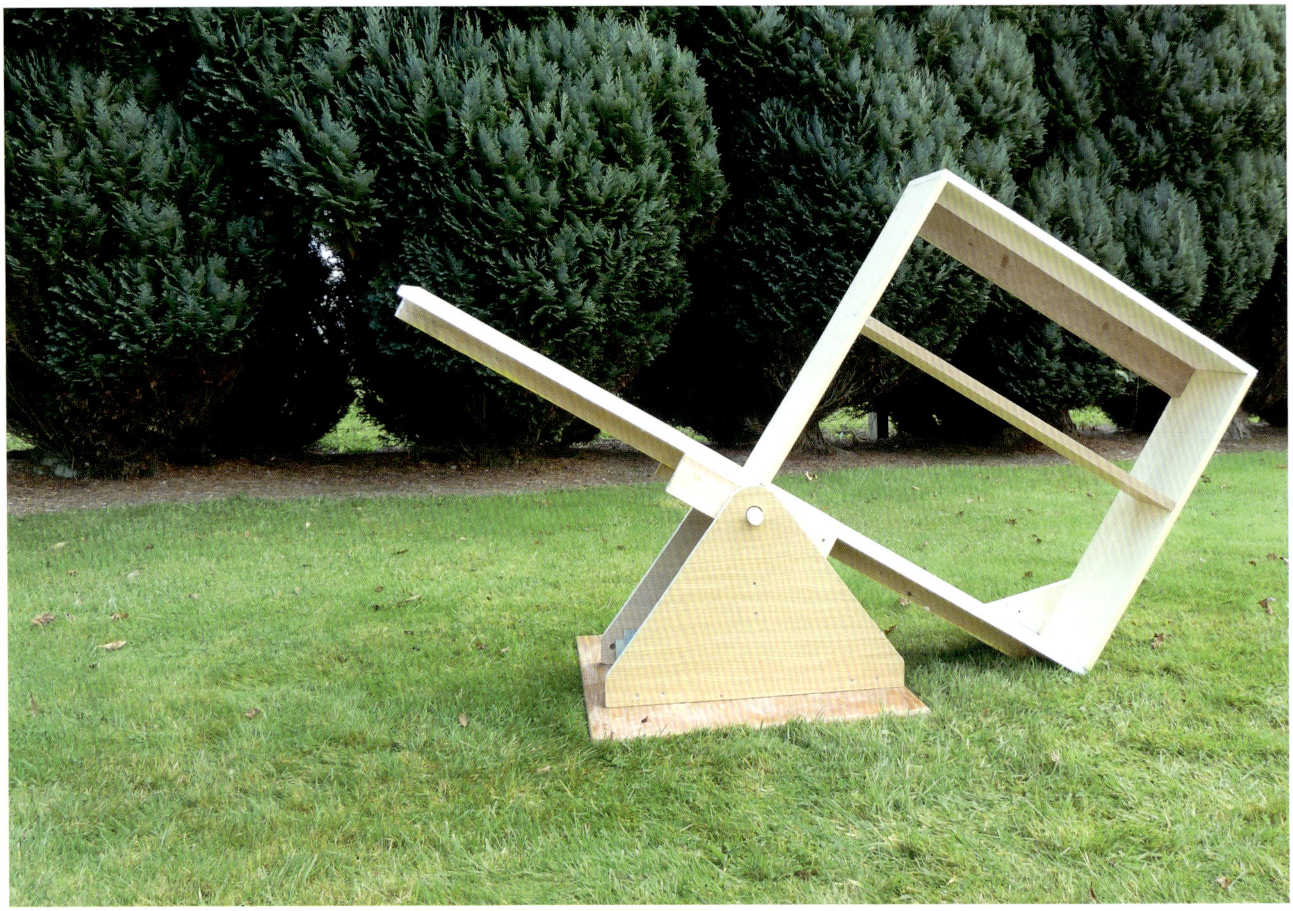

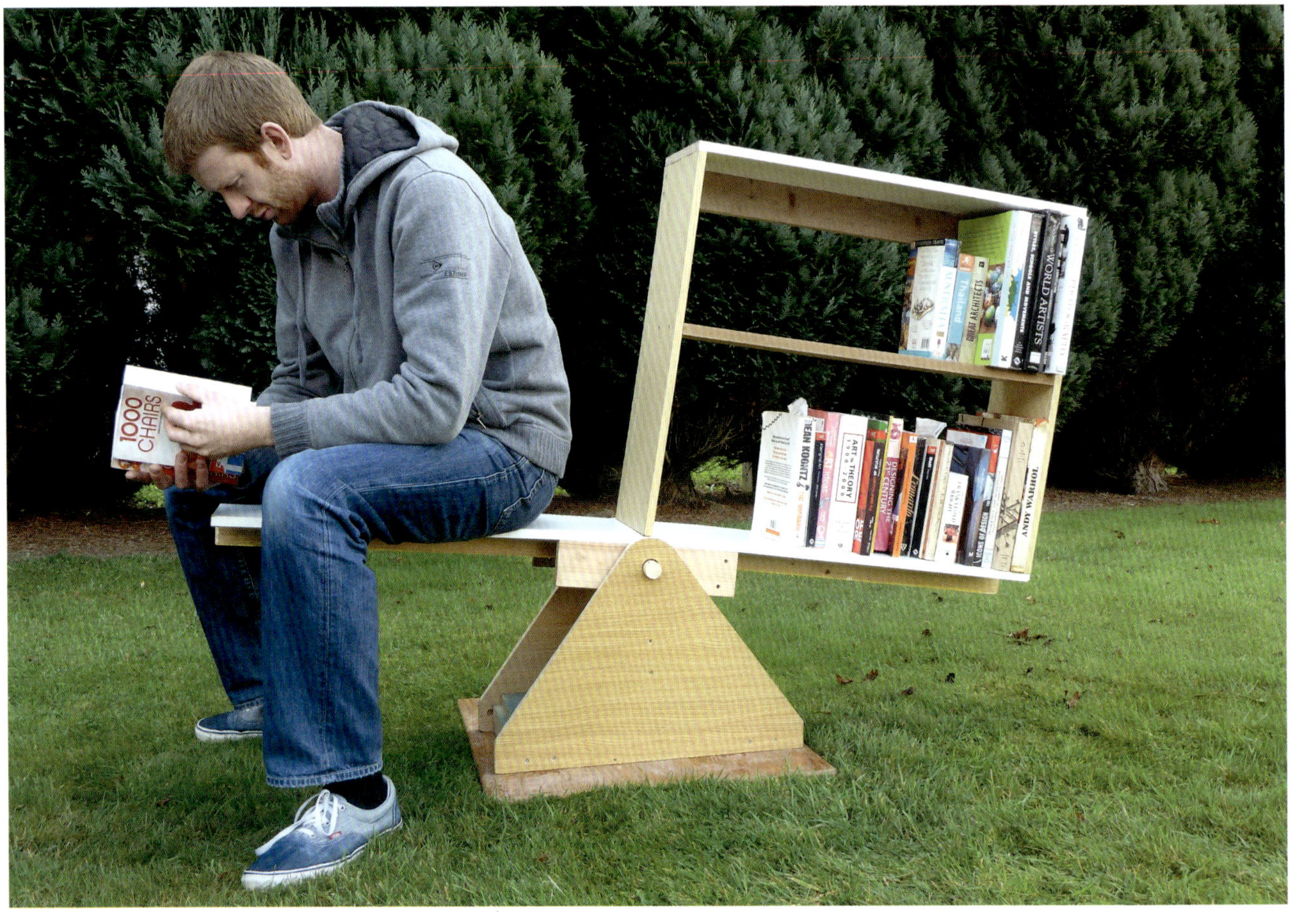
1000 CHAIRS
WORLD ARTISTS

SEE SAW SHELF

» Darragh Casey
» UK

See-Saw Shelf reflects designer Darragh Casey's playful approach to design thinking. Casey's work investigate stereotypes around the shelf and seeks alternative typologies outside of traditional furniture design practices. By positioning the shelf opposite the user, the see-saw becomes a seat for the user when the weight of books corresponds with the user's weight. Less intended as a utilitarian object, See-Saw Shelf is designed to challenge the user's physical relationship to the object and also subvert their understanding of the role of furniture.

THE IDEA

My father is a very practical man and constantly repairing and making things in his workshop. As a family we joke that when he doesn't have a project to work on he makes a shelf something. I think maybe the idea started from here. When I studied ceramic design in NCAD Dublin I made an installation of 80 ceramic cups, Soft Cups. They were specifically made to balance on angular shelves with no support or adhesive. I was interested in the relationship between objects, how they are stored and how this could impact the user. Objects with basic ergonomic relationships to the user fascinate me like cups, door handles, switches etc. With this in mind I enjoy the physicality of the book and the immediate access to information it offers. I think, with digital developments, books are used less and less in everyday life. Book can often be equated with knowledge, however they simply allow access to knowledge. If unread, they are just another physical object.

THE MOTION

› Hyunjin Seo
› Korea

The Motion is a bookshelf that doubles as a rocking chair. The multi-tasking bookshelf serving as a lounge chair offers a comfy seat for the user to read on it. The design keeps the shelf stable while saves space and materials.

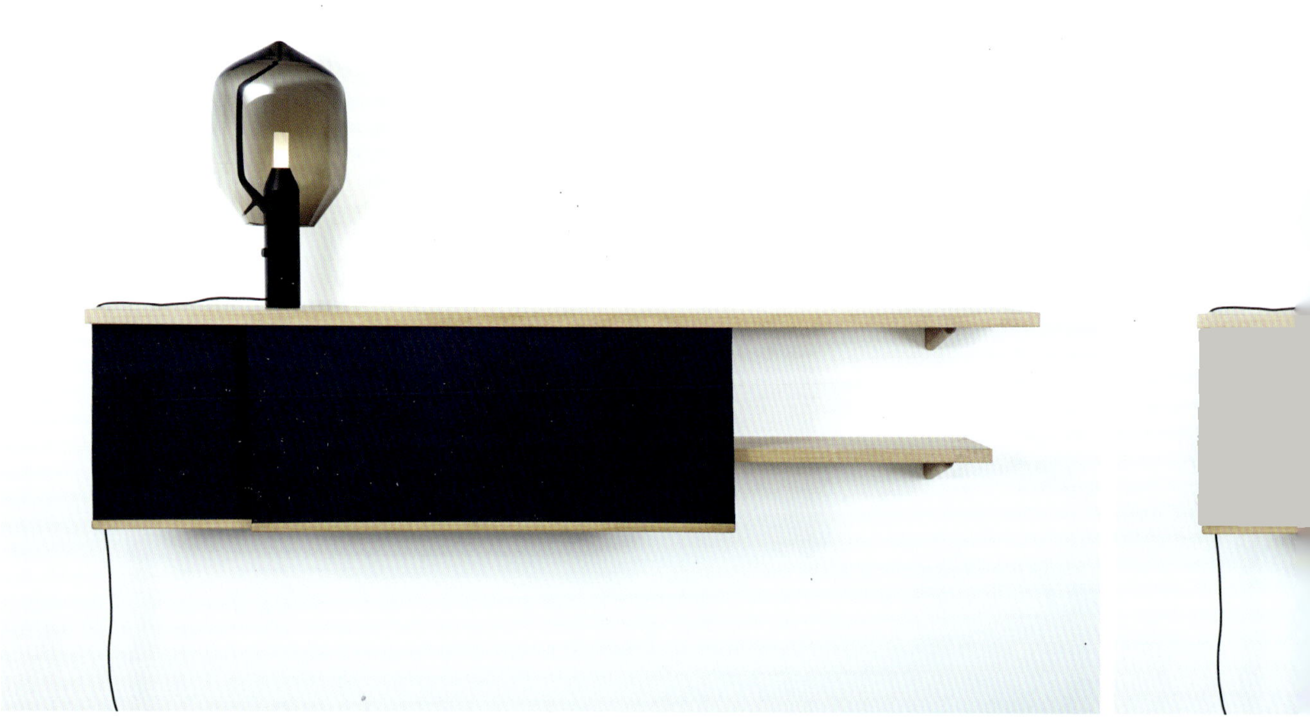

Photo ©Studio Bouroullec

FOLIO

» Ronan & Erwan Bouroullec
» France

Folio is a new type of shelving furniture that provides the possibility to hide some or all of the objects just by moving a fabric adornment that runs delicately along a discreet aluminum track.

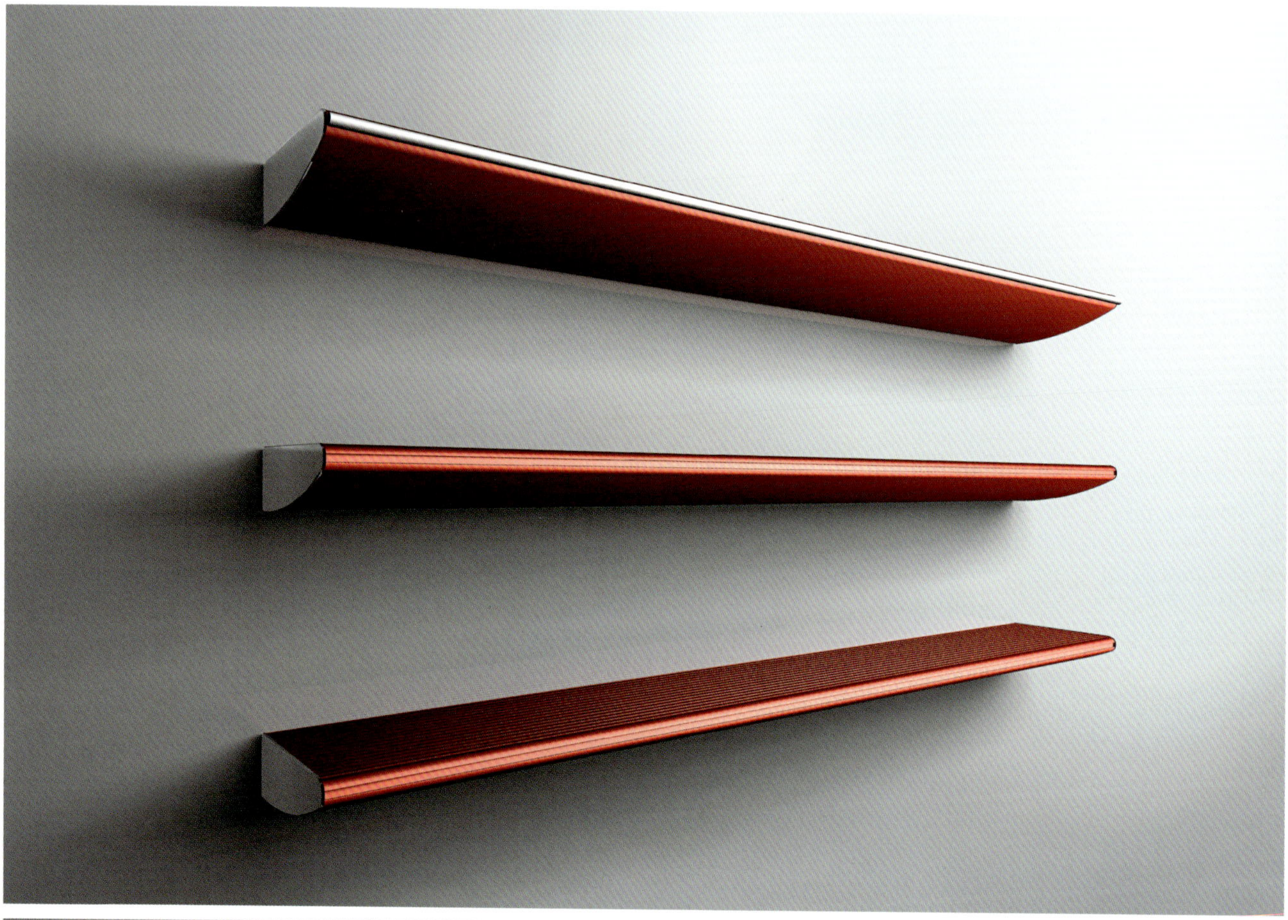

FLY

» Matteo Ragni
» Italy

Fly is a shelf with a projection screen that can be rolled down for presentations or movies. The shelf is made of stainless steel and anodized extruded aluminum, giving the whole design a modern and minimalist look.

TAMI

» Deris Jocelyn

» France

With the use of lacquered wood and steel, Tami is a table with a book rack in the center, making it both a table and a special kind of bookshelf. The multifunction and poetic character make it a refreshingly creative piece of furniture.

Photo ©Baptiste Heller

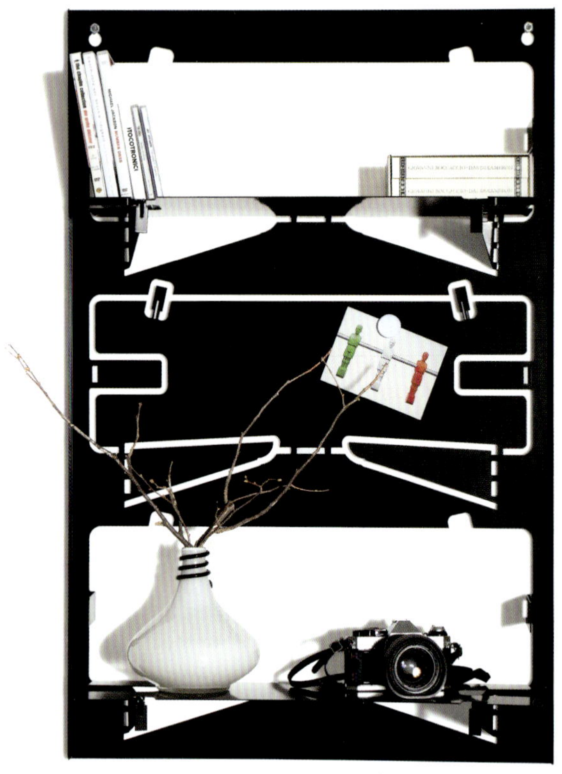

PIEGATO

› Matthias Ries
› Germany

Piegato is a single piece of laser-cut sheet steel. Perforations allow the customer to easily bend the shelf, which is delivered as a flat pack. Due to the ferromagnetic properties of the steel, the shelf can be used as a magnetic board. It is a relatively ecological product due to its efficient use of material and its recyclability.

Photo ©Matthias Ries

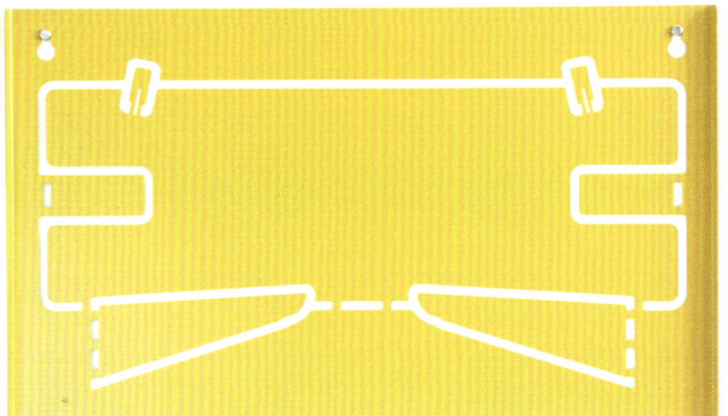

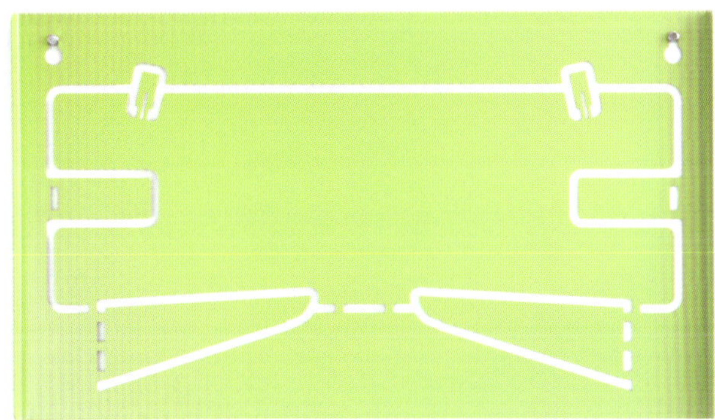

PIEGATO ONE

» Matthias Ries
» Germany

Piegato One is the little brother of the successful Piegato shelf and was released two years after the launch of the original Piegato.

BLOW

» YOY
» Japan

This project is a wall shelf that looks like a paper blowing in the wind. It is formed by curved A4-size, thin steel plates with molds. Multiple variations can be applied to the shelves which feature five different shapes. It can be fixed to the wall with a hook.

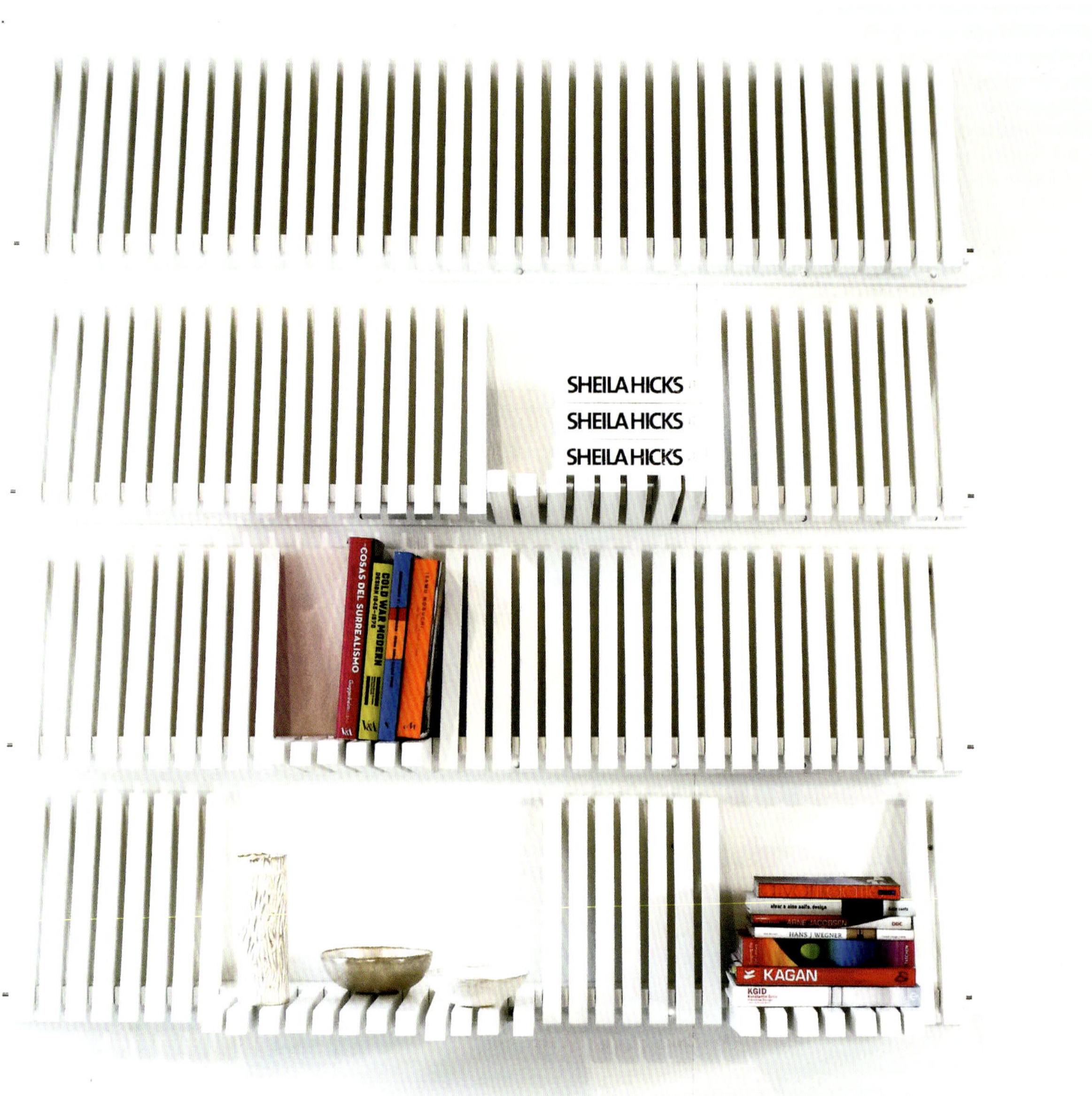

PIANO SHELF

» Sebastian Errazuriz
» Chile

The Piano Shelf allows the user to adapt and customize the shape and look of the shelf to their own needs. This shelf can function as a shelf or can be used to frame objects or books.

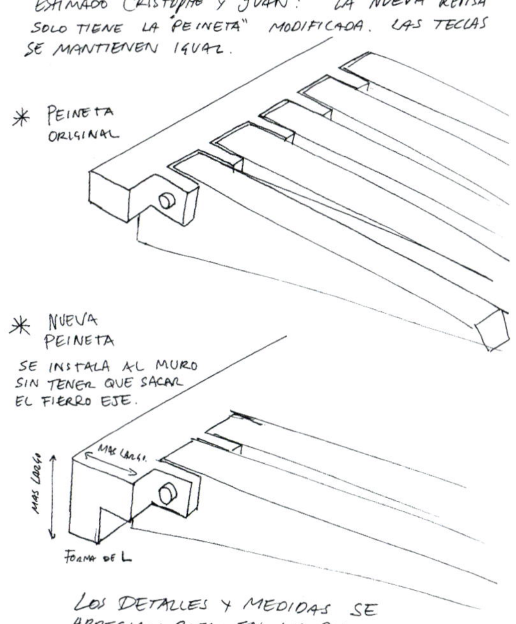
ESTIMADO CRISTOPHE Y JUAN: LA NUEVA REPISA
SOLO TIENE LA "PEINETA" MODIFICADA. LAS TECLAS
SE MANTIENEN IGUAL.
* PEINETA
ORIGINAL
* NUEVA
PEINETA
SE INSTALA AL MURO
SIN TENER QUE SACAR
EL FIERRO EJE.
MAS LARGO
FORMA DE L
LOS DETALLES Y MEDIDAS SE
APRECIAN BIEN EN LOS PLANOS.

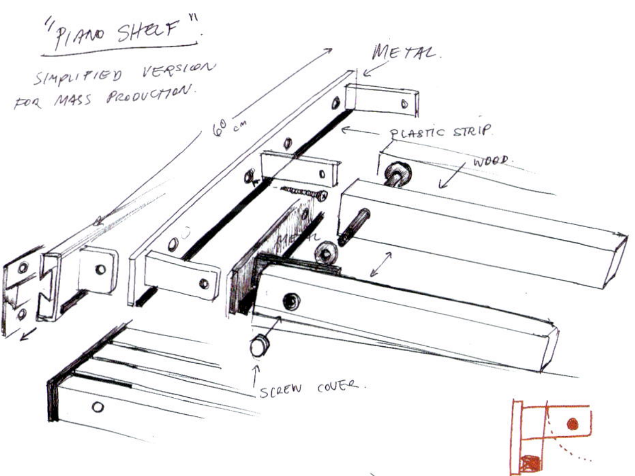
"PIANO SHELF"
SIMPLIFIED VERSION
FOR MASS PRODUCTION.
60 cm
METAL.
PLASTIC STRIP.
WOOD.
SCREW COVER.

Photo ©Chris Barnes & Lauren Cheong

CONCEAL SHELF

» Miron Lior
» USA

The Conceal Shelf transforms your books into a work of art. This powder-coated, steel floating book shelf becomes invisible behind stack of books. All the necessary mounting hardware is included.

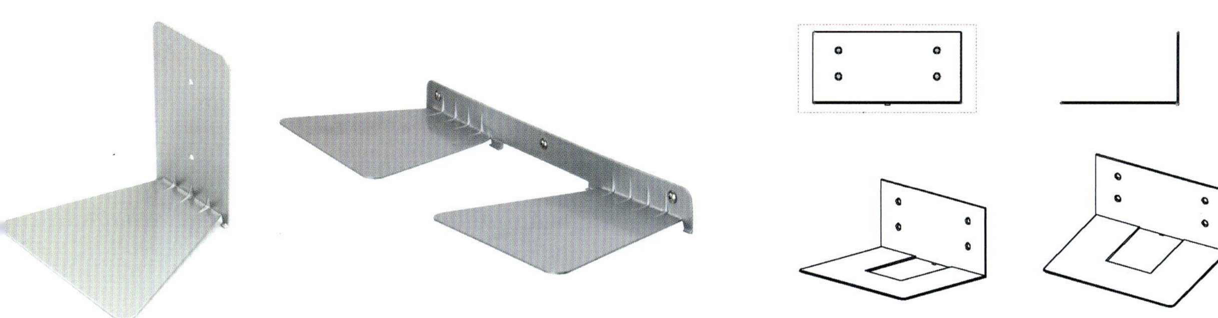

INSPIRATION

The final design is a result of conscious simplification of form until the book support disappears all together. Even though Conceal might look like it is a design revelation, in fact, it is the result of a gradual process aimed at stripping the shelf of all unnecessary parts. There are at least three other earlier versions that led to this final one. While there is plenty of minimal design surrounding us today my appreciation for minimalist style comes from the works of mid-century architects, particularly Ludwig Mies van der Rohe. His motto "Less is more" describing his aesthetic vision summarized my own views. This motto streamlined my design thinking.

WESTERN MINIMALISM & JAPANESE MINIMALISM

Japanese minimalism is different from western minimalism. Japanese design is so natural that it is not even a style but a way of life. It has this poetic quality where you could sense the deep roots within. Western minimalism can be very creative but rarely as genuine. It tries to reinvent but you can still sense the effort invested. Japanese design doesn't reinvent, but continuously evolves.

ESKIMOMÄRCHEN

GROWING CABINET

› Yi-Cong Lu
› Germany

There are moments when works and folders keep piling up in front of you, but also times when everything can be cleared quickly and smoothly. With this design people can pull out the drawers to expand the storage when needed. In doing so, the user can change the size and the shape of the cabinet.

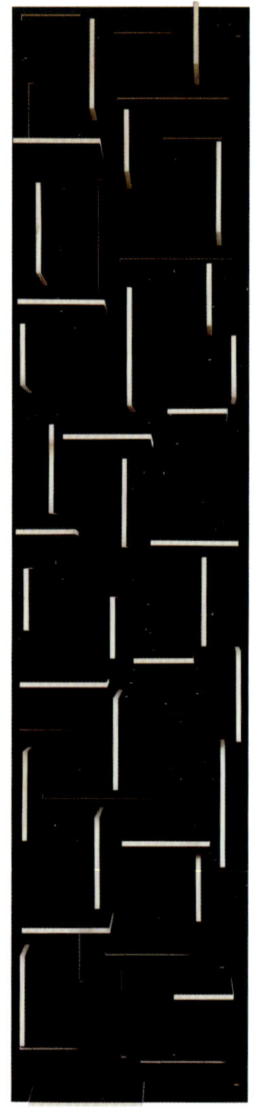

ECM
Sleeves of Desire

Barbara Wood
Himmelsfeuer
Roman

INSERT COIN

› Eva Paster, Michael Geldmacher
› Germany

Insert Coin is a customizable wall panel storage unit which is a puzzle and a bookshelf. The painted birch plywood wall panel has been fashioned with an assortment of slots that allow the user to customize the layout of the supportive tray elements, which are strong enough to hold small objects and books, offering different combinations for display.

Photo ©Nils Holger Moormann GmbH

BRAND BRAND

» Hideaki Asaoka
» Japan

Hoping children would enjoy reading books more than playing video games and toys, the designer created a bookshelf that brings more fun and enjoyment to reading. Brand Brand was inspired by one of the popular playground equipment, the seesaw. It shakes when you put or take books from the cases at the bottom of the shelf. One end of the bookshelf is designed for comic books while the other end is for education books, encouraging children to balance education and fun.

知識の重さ

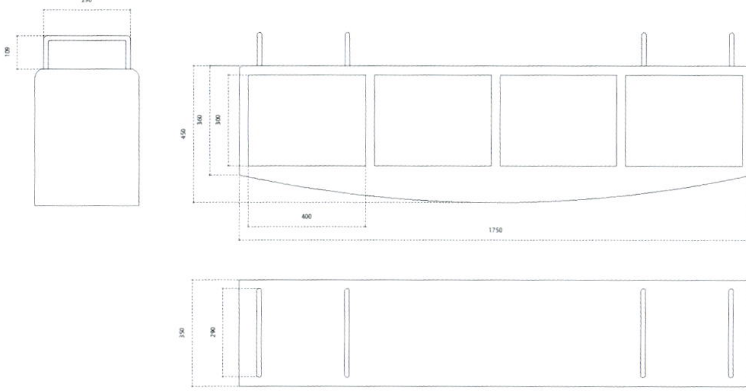
290
109
450
360
300
400
1750
350
290

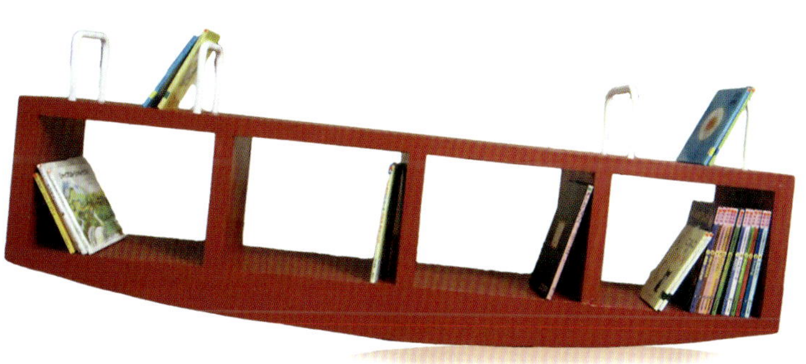

NODO COLLECTION

- Pentágono Estudio
- Mexico

The universe is full of connections. Unison is created between points to establish a balance. From this, the inspiration for NODO was drawn: a furniture collection consisting of a network with numerous connections that generate its structure and geometry. NODO takes the essence from the classic piece of furniture and transforms it into a dynamic object made entirely out of fiberglass. The interwoven fibers were not only designed to function as a structural component but to allow the piece to behave as a membrane through which communication between the environment and its context is encouraged. Instead of a solid surface piece, this product has an open aesthetic structure, displaying its content in an honest manner while using little material and maintaining high structural resistance.

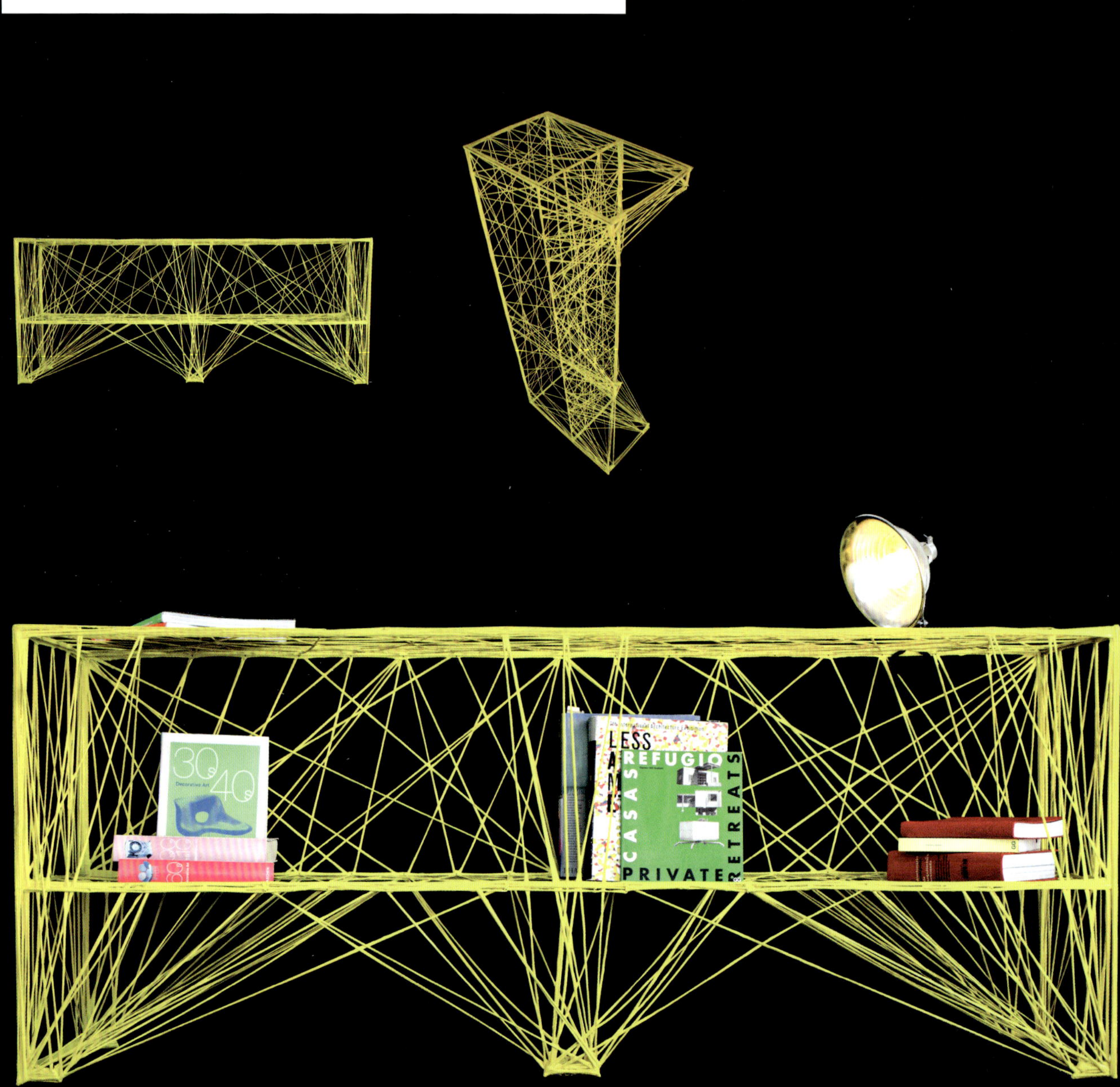

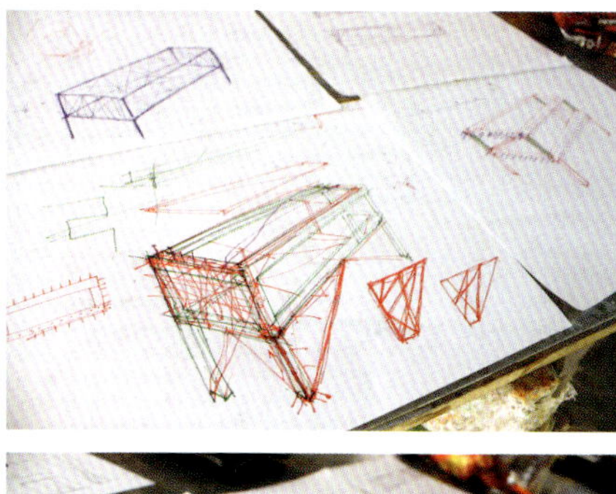

CATALYST

» Jiyoung Seo
» Korea

The beginning of a relationship involves many catalysts. Strangers can be brought together through mutual interactions and communication. This type of connection, whether done through a simple "hello" or a more elaborate activity, can be construed as a type of playful interaction. Catalyst invites the user to interact with its form. This is a shelf with an unexpected tactile sensation. Made mostly of silicon, the design has a thinner layer on the upper part that holds things like books, papers and pens, etc.

MATERIAL CENTERED

My designs are mainly expressing natural simplicity of the materials. The material that is familiar to us can open up many possibilities because it is related with people's certain behavior. That leads each user to control it with their experience. But to be succinct but also natural is my design principle.

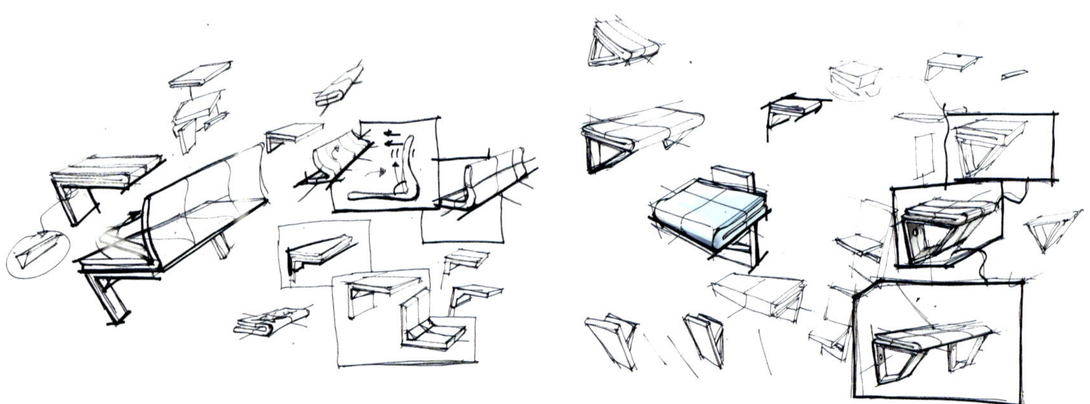

THE ABSENT
MEANING OF CONCRETE
FORM IN THEORY OF
ARCHITECTURE

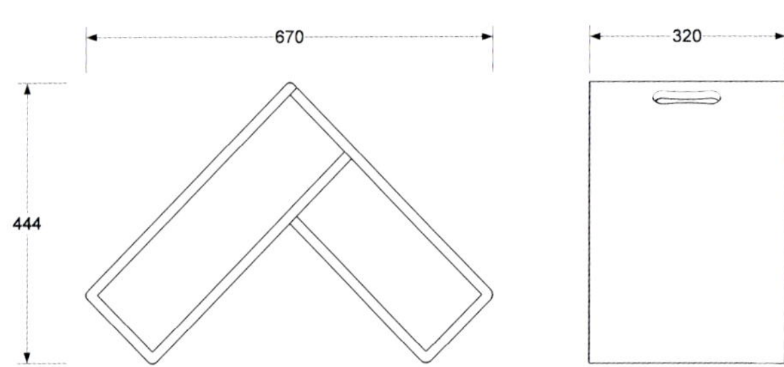
670
320
444

Photo ©Brett Rubin, Melinda Borbely

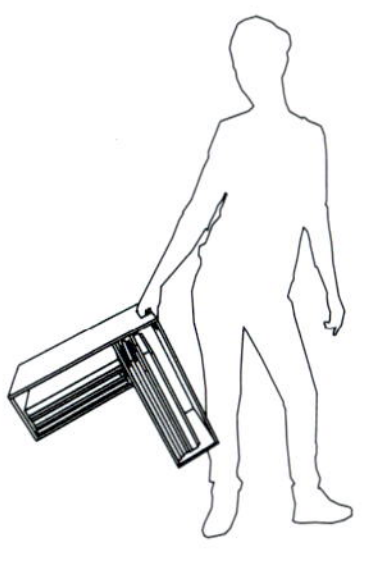

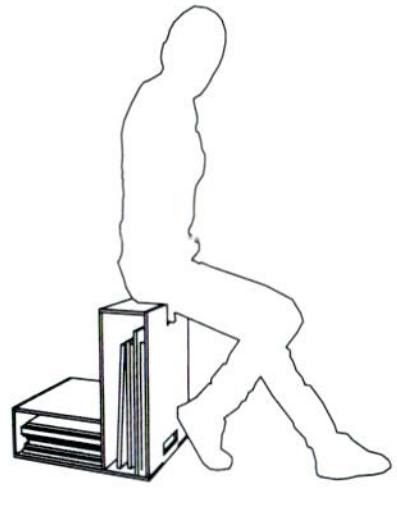

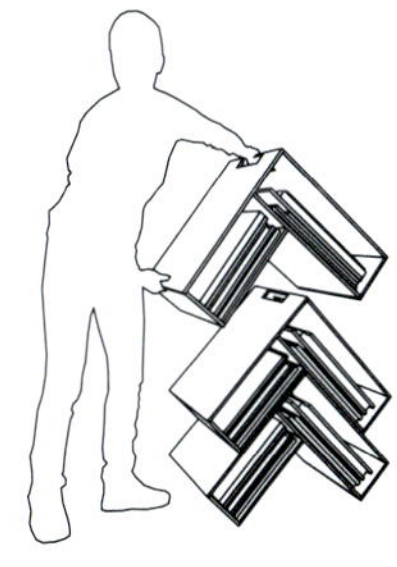

FRECCIA

› Aram Lello
› South Africa

Freccia is a new solution to store books and magazines. This project is a stackable shelving system that allows magazines or books to remain at an angle of 45 degrees, perfect for protecting the corners and sides of their covers. The modularity of Freccia allows infinitive compositions. The user can easily re-configure the position of the shelves to create a shape that changes and adapts to different needs. The initial prototypes were made of wood but the final design was produced in perspex. Each shelf is made from a single strip of perspex minimizing joints and strengthening the structure.

Photo ©Jean-Luc Abraini

MAGNETIC SPIRIT

› Benoît Bayol
› France

The designer created an unconventional tailor-made bookshelf. Its uniqueness springs from its aesthetic elegance, the efficiency of design and the values of innovation. Its components, with a patent magnetic fixing system, are easy to transport. The different compositions of this product can continue indefinitely and offer a constant reinvention of the home.

TOTEM BOOKSHELF

» Antonio Lauriola, Vito Vero / LI VING design studio

» Italy

The bookshelf is composed of three vertical modules, three "ribs" connected with a big, horizontal oak shelf. The latter is "burnt" with sodium hydroxide, creating a stark contrast with the mat lacquering of the vertical elements.

WELTFELD

» Matthias Ries
» Germany

The "Weltfeld" storage system was developed during the designer's product design studies. Years later the project continued to make an impression in different exhibitions. However, it remains to be an unfinished product open for more possibilities.

100 MAISONS POUR
100 ARCHITECTES
O ASSASSINO INGLÊS
1000
Manfrotto

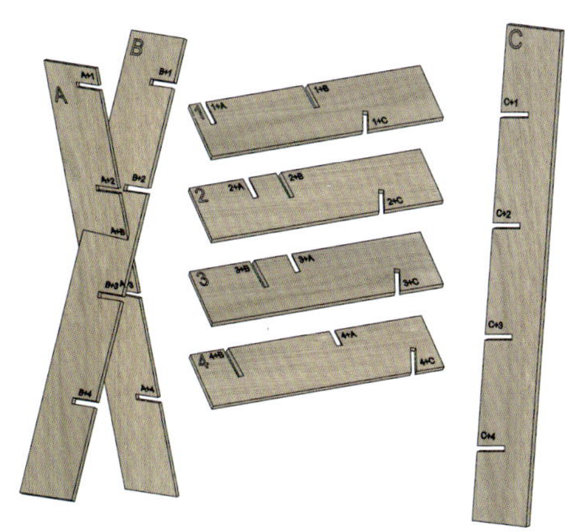

XI BOOKSHELF

» Chan Hwee Chong
» China

Like a wooden puzzle, the elaborately placed fittings allow parts of this bookshelf to lock together. Without the use of any screws or fixtures, its assembly becomes very easy. The carving of the assembly instructions on the boards shows the most technical part of the design and is present throughout the shelf's use. It also allows for taking apart and rebuilding the bookshelf anytime, since the instructions will not get lost. Despite its modern look, this shelf is very sturdy, because the X-shaped structure and the suspended vertical support hold the loose ends of the horizontal parts.

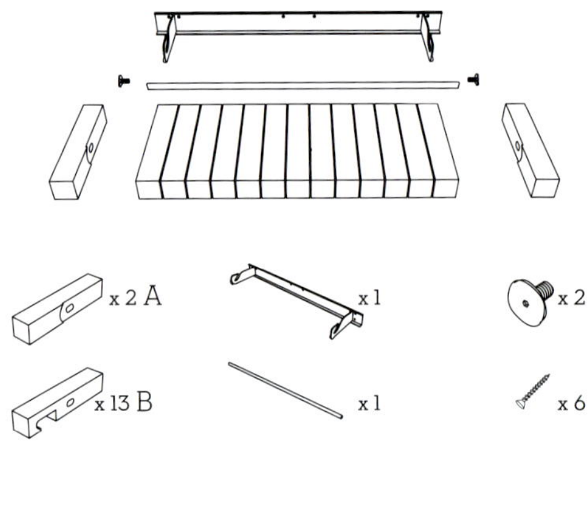

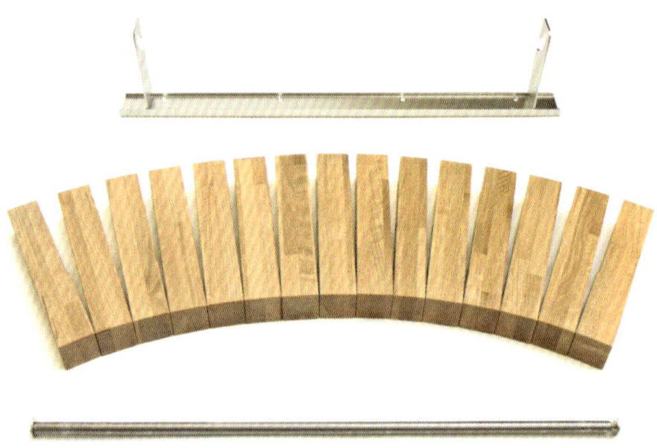

FUSILLO

› F.Cazzulo, S.Nunziato
› UK

Fusillo is an artistic piece made of polished stainless steel and solid oak in modular elements. All the modules are designed to rotate around a central axis providing support for the books. The bottom part can be used as a hanging device. With this design, multiple shelves can be customized to create new combinations according to different needs.

IL CUCCHIAIO D'ARGENTO
YOTAM OTTOLENGHI
PLENTY
River Cottage Veg everyday!
Time Out London Eating & Drinking 2005
JAMIE'S 30-MINUTE MEALS
GORDON RAMSAY'S ULTIMATE COOKERY COURSE
JAMIE'S 15 MINUTE MEALS

SHELF OF SHELVES

- Hans Tan
- Singapore

This undecorated shelf is composed of four independent units of proportionately diminishing sizes. Each unit suggests a distinctive content by describing its own space and may be repositioned to create varying configurations.

FLEXI TUBE – SHELVING SYSTEM

» Doris Kisskalt
» Germany

FlexiTube is a mobile, flexible system which can partition a room into different spaces. This fantastic tube rolls and fits into any corner and changes into a sculpture of a shelf. Inside each tube is a shelf for storage which serves as a visual horizontal line. FlexiTube is available in two different sizes and can be combined in any number either lying side by side or on top of each other. The FlexiTube sculpture can be set up in many ways even without the support of a wall.

Photo ©Andy Brunner

Photo ©Carolijn Slottje

OH

» Gerard de Hoop
» The Netherlands

OH is a versatile piece of furniture that can be used standing up or lying down, used as a side table or cabinet. It is an exceptional place for books, magazines, records, DVDs and other items. By arranging the cabinet in multiple possible variations, one can create a unique, custom wall unit.

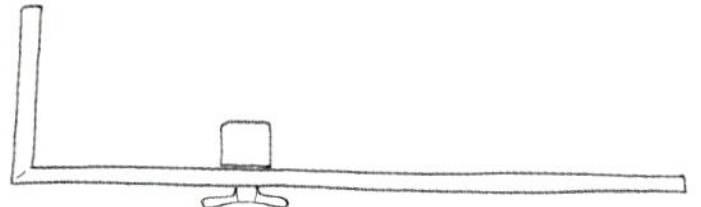

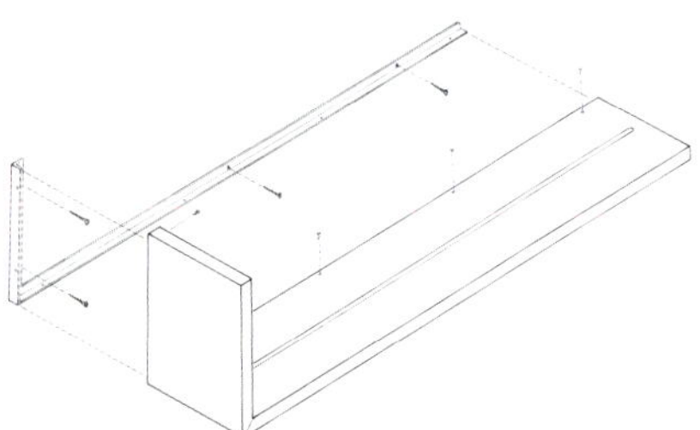

HOLD ON TIGHT

› Colleen Whiteley, Eric Whiteley
› USA

With this shelf, your books are no longer in danger of toppling over. Oversized wing-nut allows bookend to slide into place and be secured wherever needed. The design of this bookshelf was developed as a solution to problems users were facing. When in need of a handy place to keep books and sketchbooks it is often hard to find any bookends that can hold up large stacks of publications. The bookend on the shelf easily adjusts to hold your collection, whether the shelf is fully occupied or not.

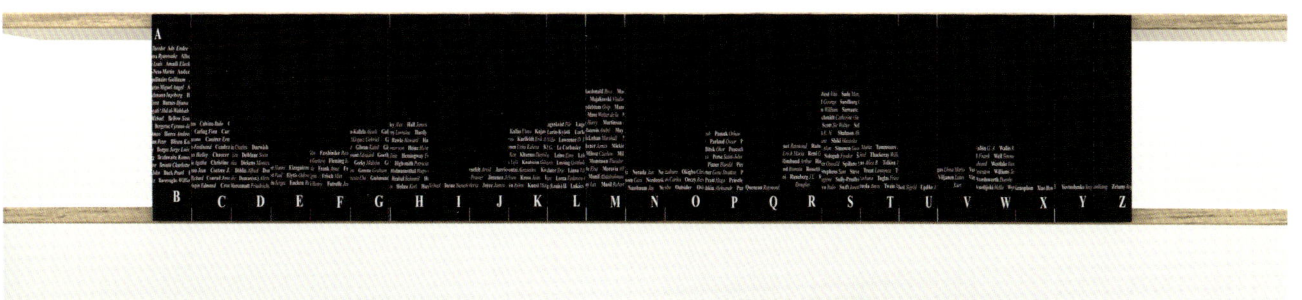

Photo ©Alvin Low

DIVIDER BOOKSHELF

› Mat Foley
› Australia

This project was inspired by a friend's obsession with book collecting. As books are rapidly becoming digital, keeping paper books will become a collector's interest. This divider bookshelf helps book collectors with organizing their collection. The bookshelf is delineated alphabetically by dividers. Each divider represents a letter of the alphabet. The dividers are inscribed with a list of authors and become a part of the structure of the bookshelf. They can be adjusted horizontally, depending on the number of books by the authors of that letter.

GIRO ONE 360°

» Juil Kim
» Korea

The shelves can be added and their height adjusted by spinning them up or down a central pole with two LED lights fixed on top. The bottom shelf can serve as a coffee table with the added convenience of having magazines right next to you. Having the Giro One by your reading chair, books and magazines are within easy reach. The unique shelf contains modules that twirl up and down and can be adjusted to varying needs. It will turn into a side table when the shelf is set low enough. Modules can be added to make more space.

BOOKSHELVES

» Kylie Vickers
» UK

The Bookshelves was a response to a study of how and where people interact with other objects in relation to the physical act of reading. As a new way to explore book storing, the range of shelves investigates the users' needs and each shelf solves a problem with a simple slot detail.

Berenice Abbott
FILM EDITING

Gabriele Basilico
LIMELIGHT
Berenice Abbott

CORNICHE MINI

» Ronan & Erwan Bouroullec
» France

Corniche illustrates the idea of creating an impromptu storage area. The idea behind this design arose from the need for small storage spaces in which items could be stored at a moment's notice. Corniches are individual protrusions in a living space that can be used and organized freely to put daily use items at your fingertips or to make a larger installation. Glossy pedestals made of ABS come in three sizes and a variety of colors including white, black and red.

Photo ©Elisa van der Linden

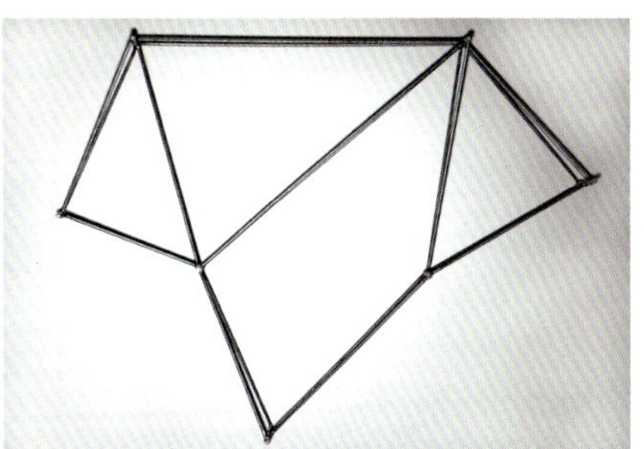

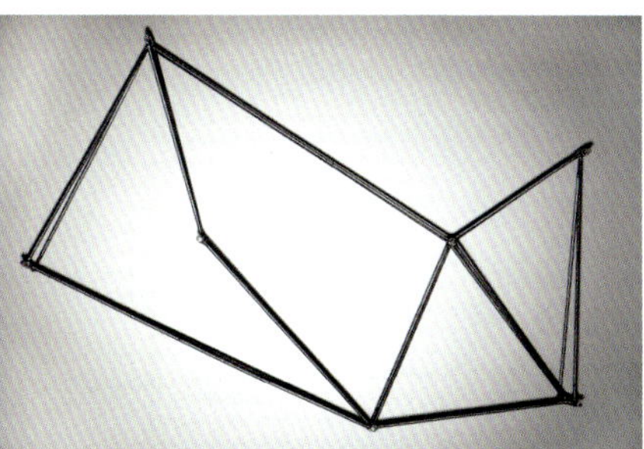

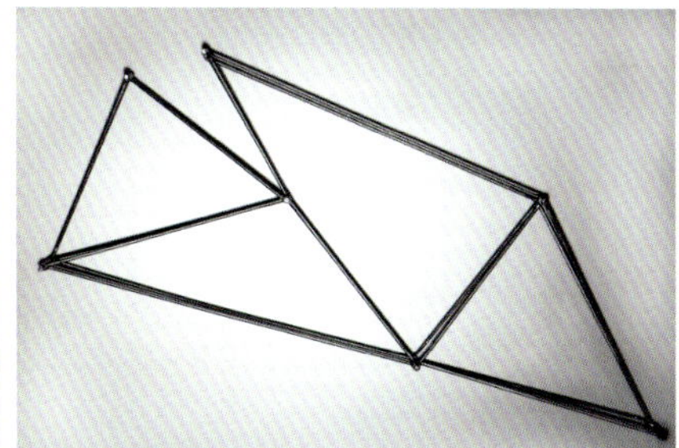

TENSOR VOTING

› Giulio Parini
› Switzerland

Tensor Voting is a mathematical algorithm to estimate various characteristics, such as dimensions and orientations, of geometrical shapes made by clouds of points. The project is a skeletal system of iron components. It consists of iron rods in varying lengths which are slotted into fasteners, and in turn are nailed to the wall. Tensor Voting allows the user to play with varying geometrical configurations by rotating the rods and switching the location of the fasteners. It can be a wall sculpture or a shelving system which can hold up a few items decently, such as paperbacks and CD cases.

Odysseus' eventyr
FRUGT HAVEN
MAGASIN
MAGASIN
Fakta

Blues
PIANO MOODS
POP SINGER

Photo ©Laura Stamer

HJORRING CENTRAL LIBRARY

» Rune Fjord, Rosan Bosch
» Denmark

A vision for a future library has become a reality in a new shopping mall where a new platform for communication and experience turns the library into a multifunctional experience and knowledge center. The heart and pivotal point of the new library is a physical communication structure that twists and winds its way through the library, breaking through walls, floors and bookcases.

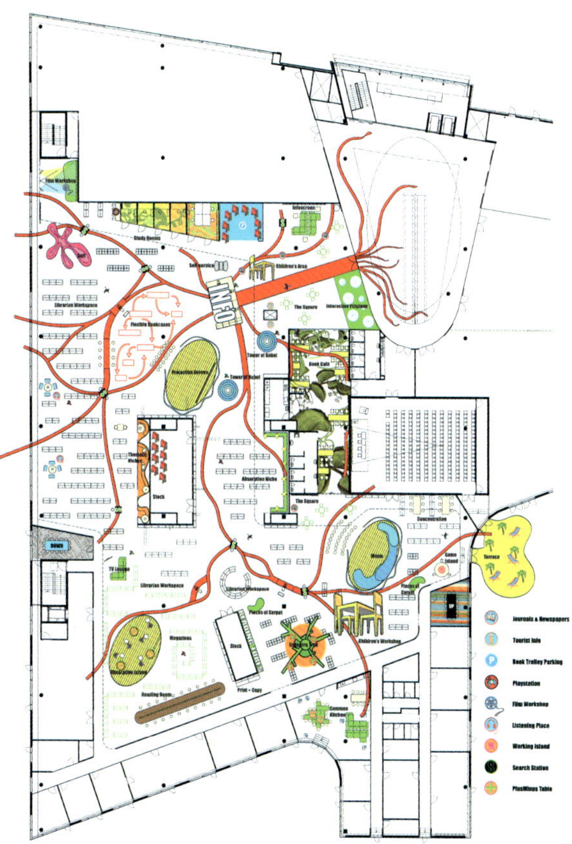

LIVRARIA DA VILA

- Architect: Isay Weinfeld
- Landscape designer: Isabel Duprat
- Graphic designer: Roberto Cipolla
- Brazil

The Livraria da Vila stands out with its pivoting window-shelf-doors. The bookshelves, which make up part of a two-story house, are certainly magnificent in their design and size.

Photo ©Leonardo Finotti

Photo ©Levitate

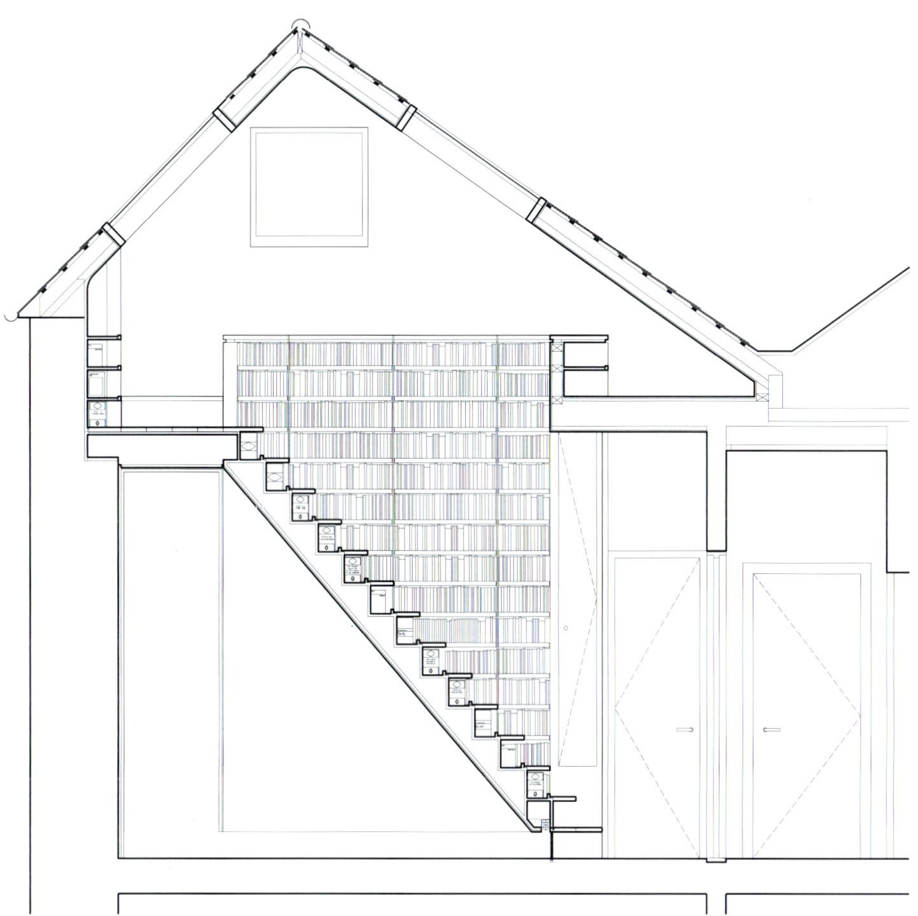

BOOKCASE STAIRCASE

» Tim Sloan, Spencer Guy
» UK

This staircase hidden from the main reception room, was created by the designers trying to access a new loft bedroom lit by roof lights. Limited by space, the designers melded the idea of a staircase with the client's desire for a library to form a "library staircase" in which English oak stair treads and shelves are both completely lined with books on three sides. With a skylight above illuminating the staircase, it becomes the perfect place to stop and browse a tome.

SAK (SOÑANDO A KURAMATA)

» Emiliano Godoy, Luis Mercado, Emiliano García
» Mexico

This design is the result of collaboration between three Mexican designers and two Finnish carpenters, under the guideline of a design by Shiro Kuramata. The bookshelf is assembled with 12 identical pieces, without any hardware or glue. Kuramata's design in 1972, a 64-square book shelf, starts with one small square shelf on one corner and finishes with a big square shelf on the opposite, creating a grid that grows in two axes. Three basic design guidelines were to take that growth to the third dimension, the depth of the shelf, to assemble the whole bookshelf by the repetition of a single piece without hardware, glue or fasteners. The bookshelf is thus flat packed. The pieces are currently manufactured by Pirwi in Mexico City in five different sizes.

Photo ©Enrique Macías

ARTERIA BOOK SHELF

- Mariano Gemmo
- Germany

For the Arteria Book Shelf, Mariano Gemmo pushed the limits of minimalism. The shelf consists only of a 6mm precisely bent piece of round-bar steel and two eyelets fix this meandering structure to the wall. Arteria only works when it is fixed vertically to a surface. The designer made use of the widely known physical law of balance that an object slightly shifted off center and only resting on one point or one line will always tilt in one direction.

SOFTSHELF

› Yong Ju Lee, Brian Brush
› USA

Softshelf was inspired by the idea of creating a bookshelf that changes the usual grid design into something different for the customer. It is fully customizable, allowing the user to manipulate elements like the overall size of the shelf, size of the boxes, the curvature of the shelf and the stretching of the shape of the boxes. Softshelf takes advantage of the rigidity and fluidity of wood combined with the precision of CNC milling technology to create a monolithic and continuous form, sturdy yet geometrically complex and ultimately innovative.

bauhaus
bauhaus archiv magdalena droste
Artemide

THREE FOLD BOOKSHELF

» Richie Chen
» USA

With a minimal appearance, the Three Fold Bookshelf is a platform to hold books in an elegant manner to display books in a variety of sizes from pocket books to magazines.

The stylish & The intriguing

WILBUR SMITH

HOLE IN THE FLOOR

» Raw Edges Studio
» UK

Hole in the Floor consists of a series of ingenious shelving units. The design was inspired by the idea of things unexpectedly ending. Unique vertical drawers with slices at the bottom bring about the visual illusion of a hole on the floor. The designers created this product with a simplicity that creates an elegant impression. In addition, the shelves are produced in different sizes and suitable for both traditional and modern interiors.

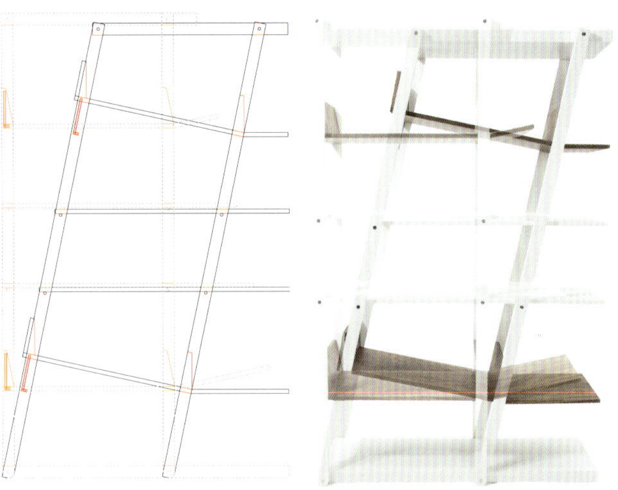

KIPPIS

• Nina Farsen, Isabel Grupp
• Germany

Without a stabilizing cross joint, a shelf is shaky and can easily lose balance. As a result, movement is made possible and the shelf tilts to the side. The overhang which is created can be used for new purposes. A mixture of pivot points and firm connections enables some shelves to keep their horizontal position while others follow the tilting movement. When the shelf is in the upright position, the sideboards of the brown distorted planks serve as chutes for papers and magazines. When it's tilted, these elements swing horizontally while their counterparts tilt at angles and form a sloping tray for books. The rotary bedded shelves stay horizontal in any position.

Photo ©Andreas Velten

PLATZHALTER

» Nina Farsen, Isabel Grupp
» Germany

Platzhalter supports weight and makes space for more books by "bursting". An initially hidden board stretches between the split halves and widens the usable surface. The more books are added to the shelf, the wider it opens. The classic rectangular shape turns into a v-shaped outline until the shelf reaches its defined limit.

Photo ©Andreas Velten

PERFECT IMPERFECTION

The bookshelves "Platzhalter" and "Kippis" are both part of a project named InVALID. This project is based on a very conceptual and experimental approach. The idea of invalidity served as a designing strategy to change familiar use or to create completely new functions. We believe imperfection is a wellspring of creativity. Deviations from the norm are usually perceived as defective, but they often develop into something new. The aim was to give disability a new meaning, thereby adding value to it and unmasking normality. During this project, we interviewed impaired persons, analyzed impediments and conducted a range of physical experiments in order to transfer obvious malfunctions into something positive and valuable.

PREI

» Sandra Böhm
» Germany

Sandra Böhm's furniture series "Prei - Furniture from Recycled Paper" is a collection of small pieces of furniture with exceptional character. The furniture items consist of a mix of paper pulp to which kaolin and common wood glue are added. This pulp is poured between the loosely arranged stack of bricks. Once the material has dried, the bricks can be moved. The piece is finished. This is not only extremely simple and cost-efficient, robust and durable but even without complex programming, also infinitely variable and thus can be adjusted to various needs.

The EMPEROR of ALL MALADIES

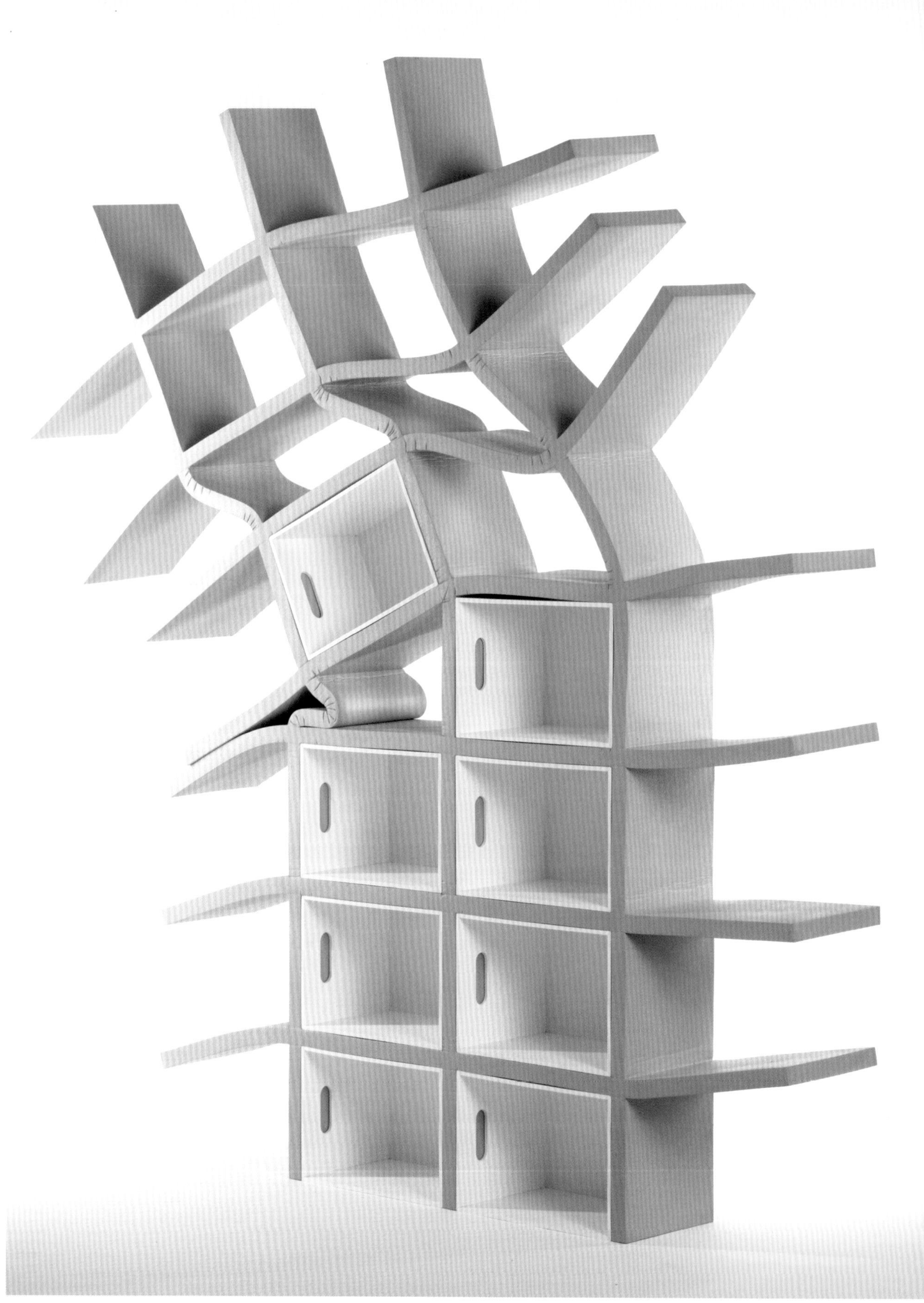

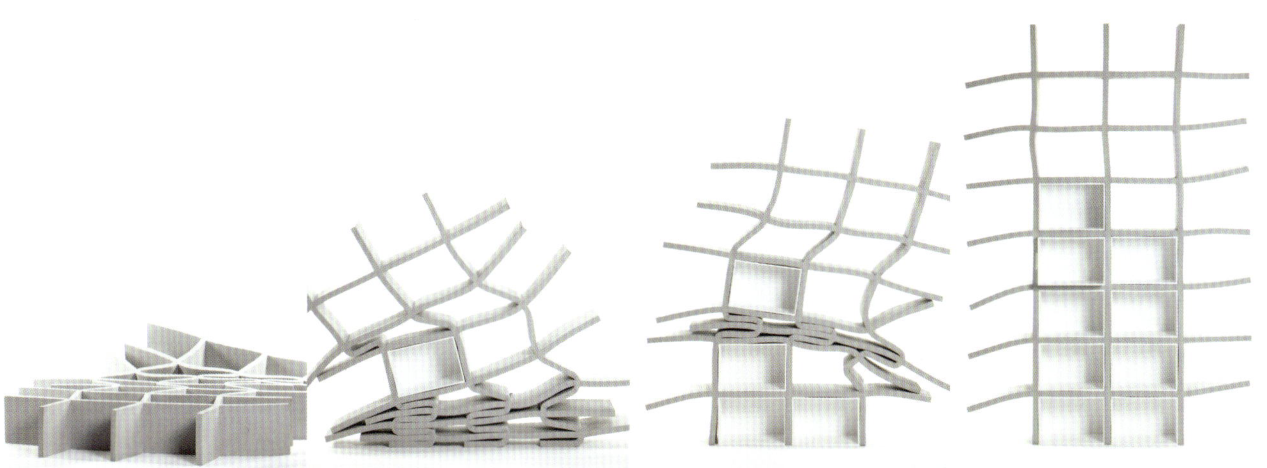

ZINFANDEL SHELF

» Tom Pawlofsky
» Germany

Designer Tom Pawlofsky confronts people with a fundamentally new concept of a shelf. Up to now, people have always thought of shelf as a stationary storage device. With its independent structure and stylistic differences, this piece of furniture is regarded as a permanently installed structure or at least as a fixed entity. The designer sees a shelf as a set of transport boxes whose main function is to hold household effects regardless of whether these are stored in one place or moved around. The soft and very light polyurethane foam grid only provides shelf compartments for the boxes. Yet its real appeal is, above all, revealed when the grid is not fully occupied.

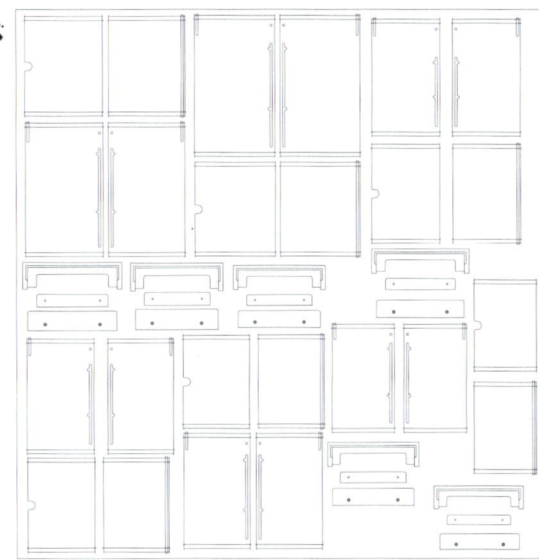

Photo ©Merlin Laumert

A BOOK BOX

› Miriam Aust, Sebastian Amelung
› Germany

A Book Box presents a beloved, yet long-unread, book mounted to the wall. Framed and exhibited, it is presented with a new functionality. Once opened, the book hides and protects the contents inside. Closing the book opens the box. The book turns into a trap door that reveals a storage area or secret compartment. The goal of designing this product is to stimulate the desire to read. It is also very easy to take the contraption off the wall and browse through your book once again.

SHELF

▸ Veronika Paluchová
▸ Slovakia

This shelf, titled simply "Shelf", displays the power of nature. The branch of a tree actually forms part of the bookshelf. In the middle, it breaks and lifts upwards. Each shelf is original, because in the wild it is impossible to find two identical branches.

Photo ©Yasuko Furukawa

EXTEND

» Naoki Ono, Yuki Yamamoto / YOY
» Japan

Extend is a bookend on which books can be placed at an extension of a desk. It can be fixed to a tabletop by a clamp and the length can be adjusted. It is formed by bending a 2mm steel plate in order to make it strong enough to support the books.

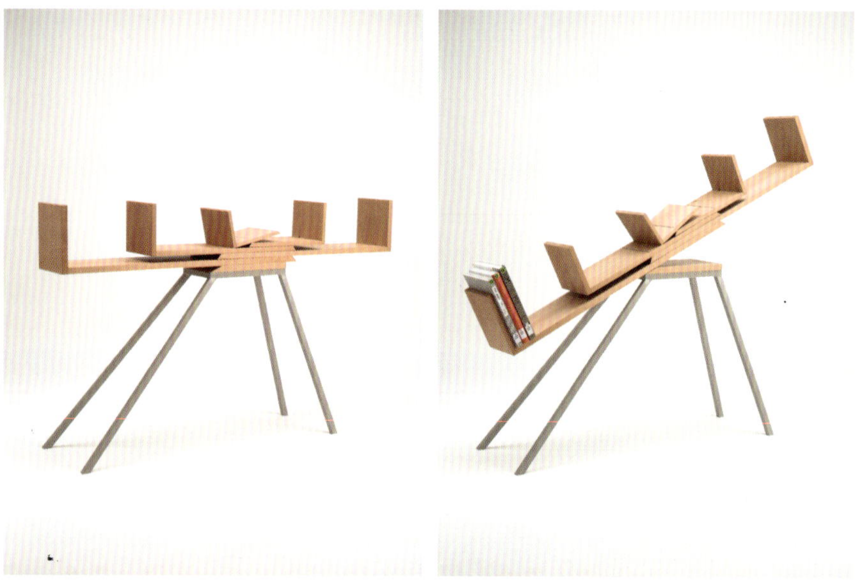

APPLAUS

• Cindy Strobach
• UK

This bookshelf explores the balance in furniture design. The proportion and position of the five boards are not coincidental but the result of calculations and experiments through which the user reaches an understanding of balance. The shelf is made out of beech, coated metal and upholstered thread which is used for connections. Boards are connected by stitching, reminding one of the ligation of books. Every board is stitched to the bottom of another piece. The "ligation" serves the functions as hinges. The immediate impact and impression reflect the designer's determination to challenge gravity.

TAKING ART
TURNING PAGES

Photo ©Matt Innes

BOOKS SHELF

▸ Matt Innes, Saori Kajiwara
▸ Australia

As printed books seem to be disappearing, the printed books that people are still reading are becoming more precious and deserve a respectful place in our homes. With that in mind, the designers worked on a bookshelf that would fit books that we go back to from time to time. It should be able to fit some big design books, novels, pocket-size mangas and perhaps a few magazines.

PACK OF DOGS

• NEL Colectivo
• Mexico

These pieces were designed by the Mexican collective NEL, and are based roughly on the shape of a dog, in different sizes and positions. The different dogs, named after famous Mexican wrestlers Dos Caras Jr., Aguayo, Superastro, El Santo, Alushe and Místico, may be placed in your house or office and serve as a side tables, stools, benches, bookshelves, magazine racks, newspaper holders, bookends, etc. The pieces are made using traditional woodworking techniques, using FSC certified young teak. Every piece is assembled from pieces of different sizes and colors, making each of them unique.

Photo ©Dante Busquets

KENN BRUTAL

» Kenyon Yeh
» Chinese Taipei

For this particular shelf system, the cutting technique is unique along with the way to connect all the pieces into one large piece. That is what makes Kenn Brutal unique and original–the way it reinforces the impression of natural decoration in the house. An important element incorporated into the design is the traditional English chair legs, recomposed to hold the whole structure.

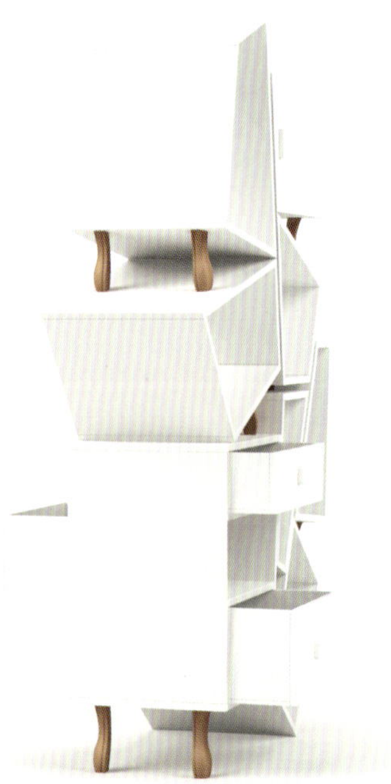

CHOPPED TREE BOOKSHELF

- Lenka Czereova
- Slovakia

This small bookshelf interprets the moment when a tree trunk is chopped down and falls to the ground, reconstructing its natural stiffness. Flexibly, the furniture is composed of four elements that can be stacked and fixed on each other or used individually.

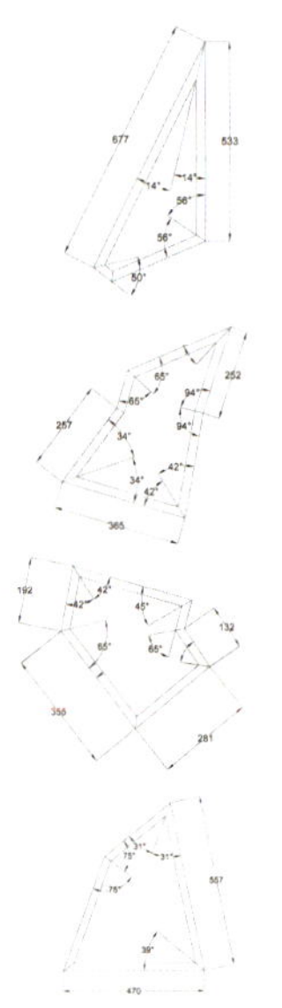

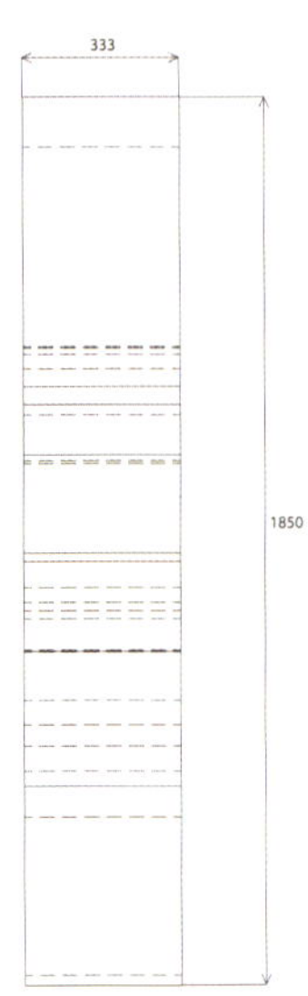

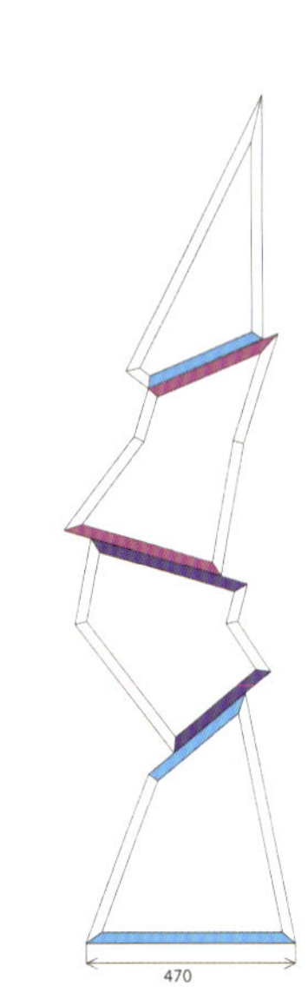

FOER
Dieter Rams:
As Little Design as Possible
Sophie Lovell
murakami ego

Photo ©Jean Pelle

ENTRY & BEDSIDE CONSOLES

- Jean & Oliver Pelle
- USA

These consoles are designed to take up little space while offering a large amount of functionality. It is an ideal storage unit for smaller living spaces where one must make the most of each piece of furniture. The multiple drawers and compartments allow for the organization of all kinds of household knick knacks like keys, mails, pens, phones and chargers.

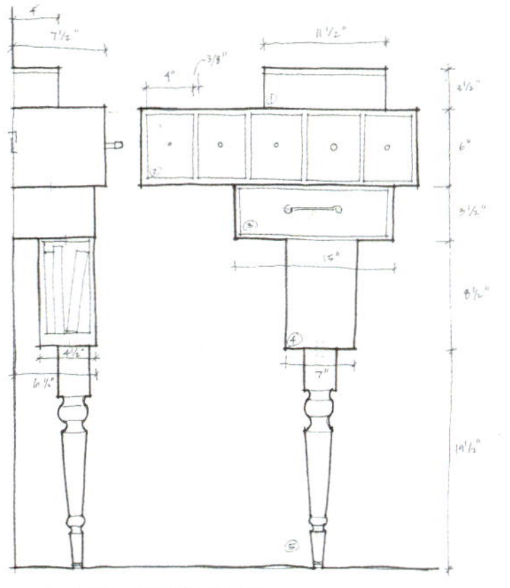

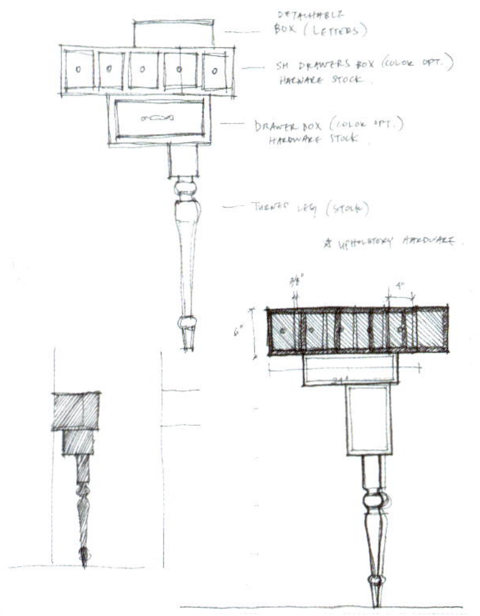

MULCIBER

» Emiliano Godoy
» Mexico

This bookshelf is made of very thin birch plywood boards, which are barely thicker than a quarter of an inch. By joining and flexing all the structural segments, the shelf gains strength for stability and resistance.This bookshelf is detachable and easily packed for transportation or storage. During assembly the user can place the shelves at different heights to accommodate books or other objects of various sizes.

Photo ©Pirwi

I like books

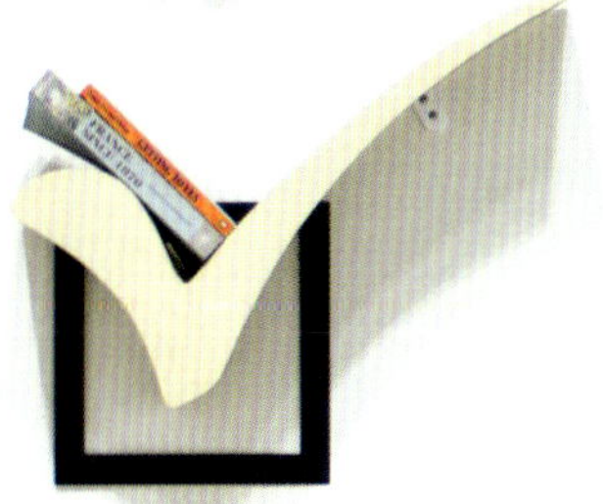

I like design

I like furnitures

CHECK

» Jongho Park
» Korea

This design reflects the meaning and importance of a book through the V-like, checkmark shape that is often used in checklists. In this case, it is used as a bookshelf. The "check" shape was made of birch plywood. By attaching the square shape made of iron, which represents a "checkbox", to the back of the wood, it clearly emphasizes the symbolism.

ABC BOOKCASE

› Eva Alessandrini, Roberto Saporiti / REdesign
› Italy

The ABC Bookcase uses a shelving system that allows users to exploit the spaces of a modern bookcase in all its potential. It is available in multiple colors, using contrasting tones on the external and internal surfaces. The bookcase is presented as an original and versatile piece of furniture.

Photo ©Roberto Saporiti

BOOKSPILE

» Andrius Pocius
» Lithuania

The inspiration for creating Bookspile came when the designer was going through his home library. He happened to rearrange his books into a huge pile and somehow its form attracted his attention. The idea was to create some shelves that would appear to dissolve amongst the books. This idea of an ideal pile was key to the decision to create an easily transformable book pile according to different needs or moods.

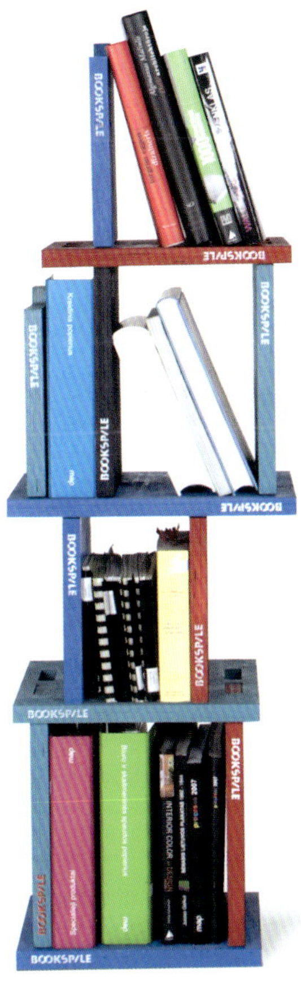

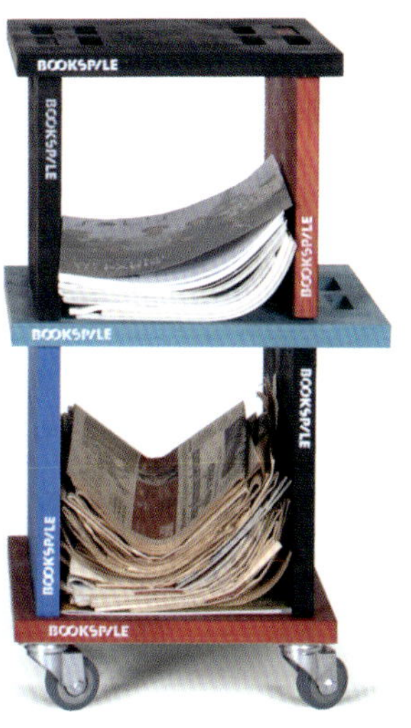

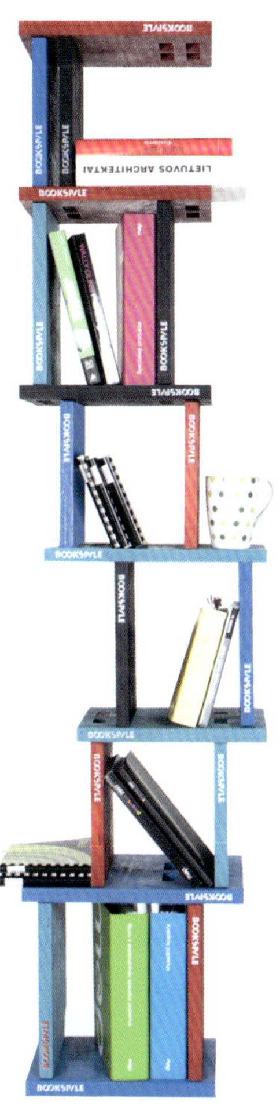

BUNGEE BOOKS

› Michel de Jesus
› Portugal

Bungee Books takes over the furniture panorama by being irreverent and bold, which offers a new way of organizing books. A minimalist shelf that is elegant and attractive, pieces up together with every new book added to the shelves. The shelf gives the user a new perspective of their books.

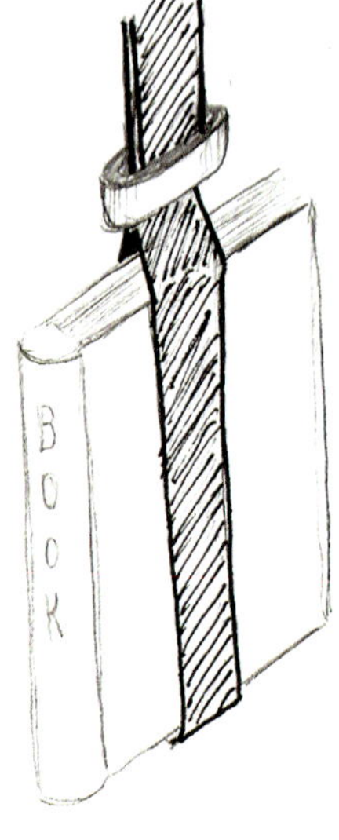

Photo ©Deadgood

DEADGOOD BOOKSHELF

› Max Lamb
› UK

The Deadgood Bookshelf features a single bar that extends from the wall and incorporates a simple U bend that offers support for your favorite book. In turn, this creates an ideal bookend to lean additional literary classics up against.

Photo ©Enrique Macias

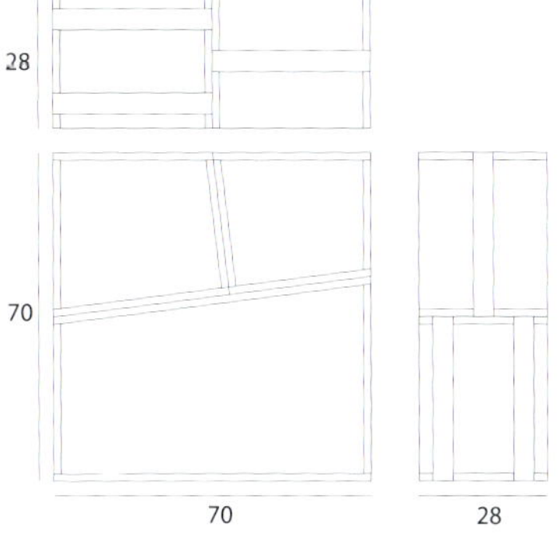

MAROMA

» Daniel Romero
» Mexico

Maroma is a modular storage unit with three slanted cubes attached to one another by means of straps that allow the cubes to rotate along two axes. Inspired by a traditional Mexican toy, this playfulness is quite surprising, permitting the user to stack more than one Maroma in several different configurations.

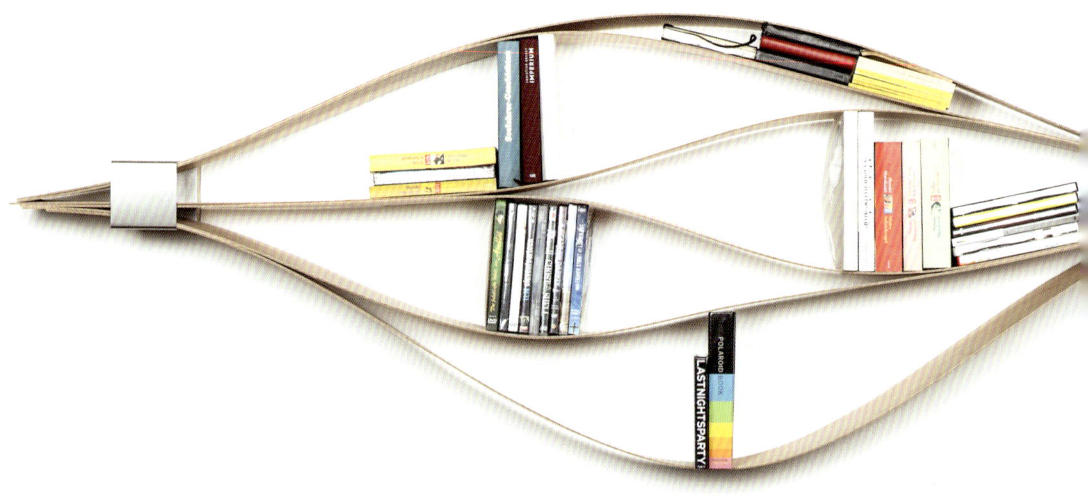

Photo ©Leopold Fiala

CHUCK - WALLSHELF

- Natascha Harra-Frischkorn
- Germany

Chuck is a shelving system inspired by the idea of creating an individually flexible room. At first glance, it is a simple wooden wall-shelf, but when you look closer, you find a shelving system made up of flexible wooden planks that adapt to the objects stored and displayed. The project consists of six wooden planks with two stainless steel, locking collars placed at the ends. Chuck makes it possible to exploit the possibilities of the elements and to design a unique room. The wood bands can be lifted separately in order to display your favorite items. Depending on the quantity of the objects, the bands stretch out and the wall-shelf takes on different shapes. The result is an intriguing interaction of flexibility and stability, a structure of rising and falling waves, which easily creates room for all of your favorite objects and books.

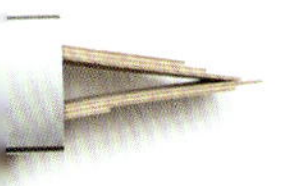

PONS
PONS

FICELLES

» Deris Jocelyn
» France

Made of wood boxes and steel wires, this furniture collection reveals the constantly hidden structure. Ficelles puts the framework in the foreground and joins it with geometric boxes. The contrasting forms and materials contribute to the design's functionality, graphic look and uniqueness.

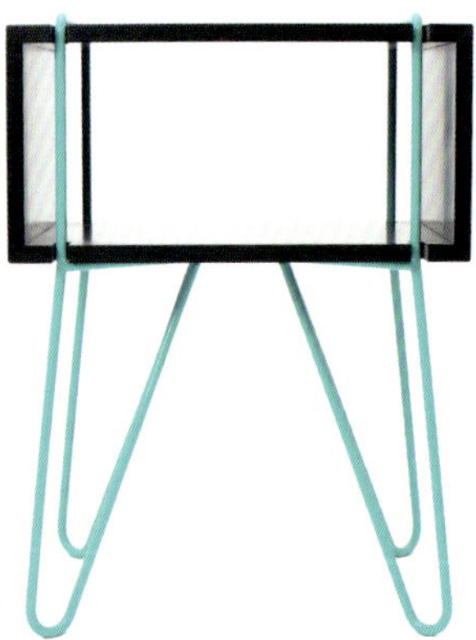

Photo ©Baptiste Heller

PITCH CONTROL

» Matt Braun
» USA

Pitch Control is a product inspired by many years of record collecting. The slight pitch allows for records, books or magazines to lean naturally and prevent warping.

THE IDEA

When a lot of records are on a shelf they start to lean on each other. Depending on the shelf, this can put a lot of pressure on the records and can warp them over time (this is also true for books and magazines). Pitch Control compensates for this natural leaning which is about 75°-85°. The principle behind this design is to have something that maximizes efficiency while being as refined and simple as possible. There is very little waste when making these and there is only one piece that is duplicated. (This decreases the energy and time needed to produce.) The geometry takes advantage of the material's thickness and provides an angle that is not too extreme and provides "extra" spaces between the modules. If the angle were less the records or books would not be stable and if the angle was more they would easily break when they are filled or when somebody sits or stands on them. The result is a product that is highly functional, environmentally conscious and aesthetically fits well in most modern interiors.

THINK GREEN

There will continue to be many different forms and concepts for all types of products. What I would like to see is more attention to the waste produced by the design industry. Taking advantage of local manufacturing, local resources, being conscious of the energy, water and other materials used to produce and distribute the finished pieces should all be considered. How all of this affects society and the environment needs to become the focus in all design.

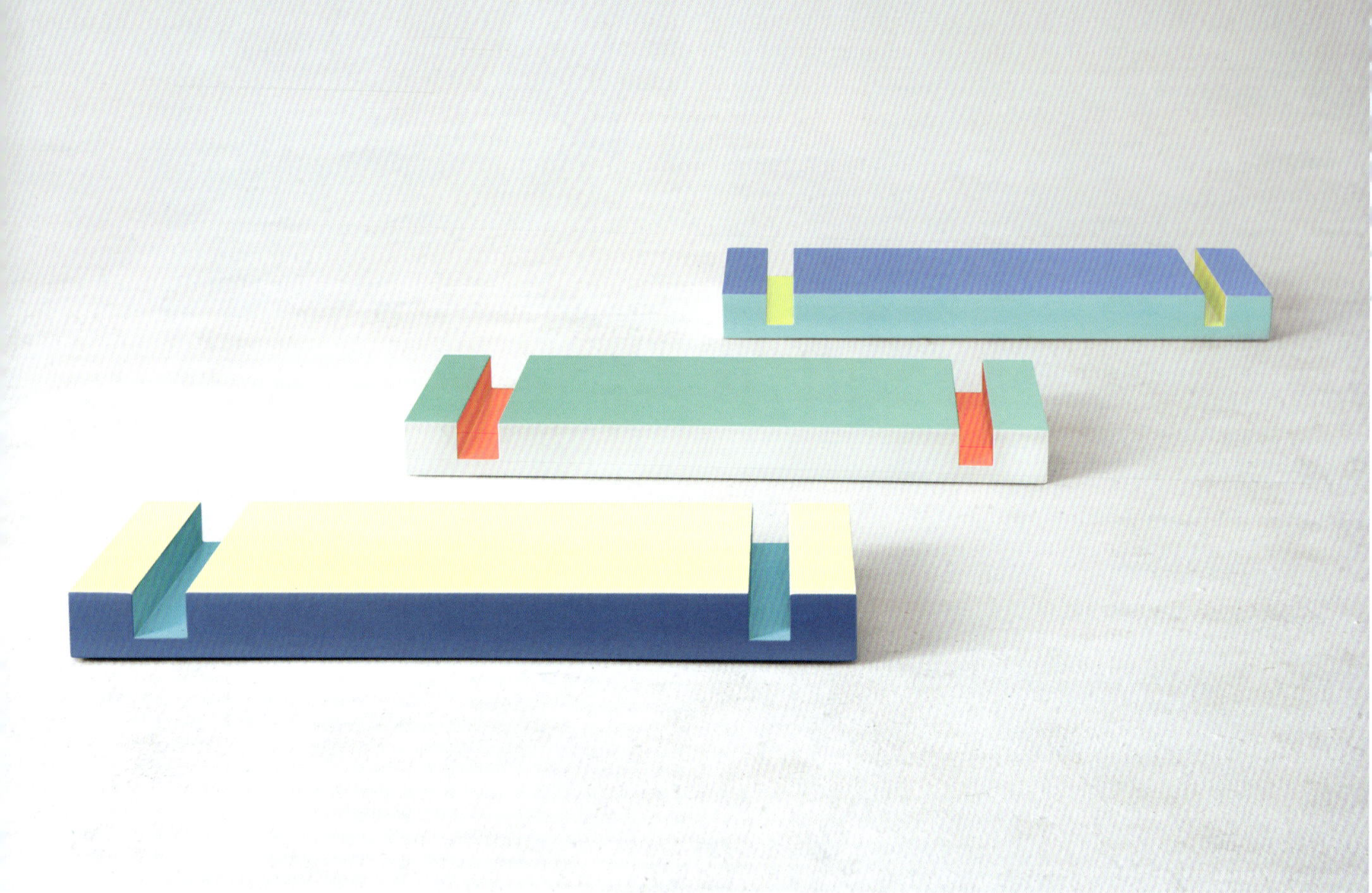

MINIMAL BOOKSHELF

» Chan Hwee Chong
» China

This bookshelf features grooves cutting into both ends of a shelf, which the user can slot books into to serve as bookends. If the book collection is too large for one shelf, a second or third can be added, with the bookends doubling as pillars to support the shelves stacked on top.

STUFFZ DESIGN ON MATERIAL
PAPER CUTTING
Illustration • Play 2
*Copywriting
a new kilo
卓越家具

STAGE DESIGN
God's Story for Me BIBLE
wok it
ROAD LESS TRAVELED
Cool Offices
TYPE
EPHEMERAL
FONTS
卓越家具

360 SHELF

› Luka Pirnat
› Slovenia

360 shelf changes the way you organize your space, books and other gadgets. With a simple built in adjustment system hidden inside, it can be adjusted at any angle to meet different needs. A zinc plated, custom made holder was developed with custom brass pin that gives you a perfect grip of objects in various shapes and sizes. The 45 degree wooden profiles inside the frame are made from solid beech wood. Manufactured with different materials in various colors, these shelves could be transformed into a beautiful installation on the wall.

Photo ©Igor Škafar Da photohouse

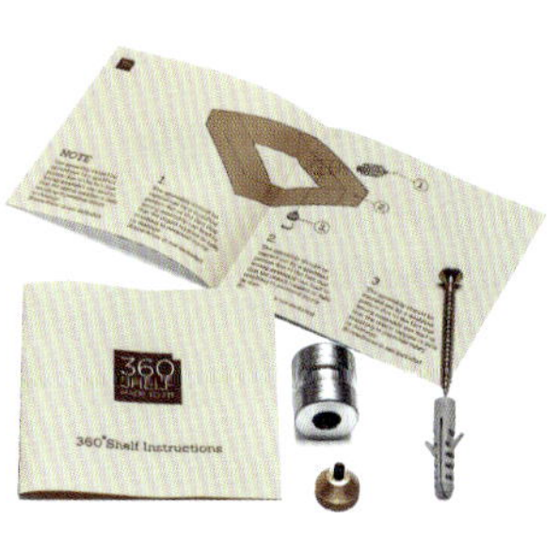

SEPARATION SHELF

- Studio Ve
- Israel

This is a shelf for couples that live together. In a regular mode, the supporters are inserted into the grooves, and serve as both hangers as well as book supports. When the couple separates, the supporters are used as working tools. Each partner takes his or her share of the common property.

SHELLF COLLECTION

» Ka-Lai Chan
» The Netherlands

SheLLf is a linguistical and conceptual amalgamation of "shell" and "shelf". Like a shell, it undulates from flatness to depth, creating a dynamic space, which is made of separate compartments that are arranged in a gently increasing and decreasing way. It seems as if the shelf is crawling across the wall, literally growing out of the wall, like an animal crawling out of shell. The cabinet's outside has a perfect smooth, glossy black mirror-like textured surface. Inside, a rough reddish, grainy, untreated wood creates a startling contrast. SheLLf is available in three sizes: small, medium and large.

B-OK

› Marica Vizzuso
› Italy

B-OK is a practical, multipurpose and space-saving bookshelf. It is a "tower" composed of four wood panels with the cross cuts of different sizes and dimensions, which allow the horizontal arrangement of books. The panels are assembled together by metal hinges on three edges while the fourth has quarter the magnets to allow the closure and stability of the bookcase. B-OK hides the screen function that could serve as divider for the living spaces within the house. Due to the panel's mobility, it is possible to place the bookshelves in different ways, in order to divide the space in different ways, with or without books. B-OK is perfect for exhibitions and it is available in different materials.

PIERO DELLA FRANCESCA
La Maschera e l'Artista
ENCICLOPEDIA DELLA GEOGRAFIA
KLIMT
GIOTTO
MANTEGNA
MONET
DESIGN IN 1000 OGGETTI
PHAIDON DESIGN CLASSICS
PICASSO
TIZIANO
Grande Enciclopedia Universale

Photo ©Joeri Reynaert

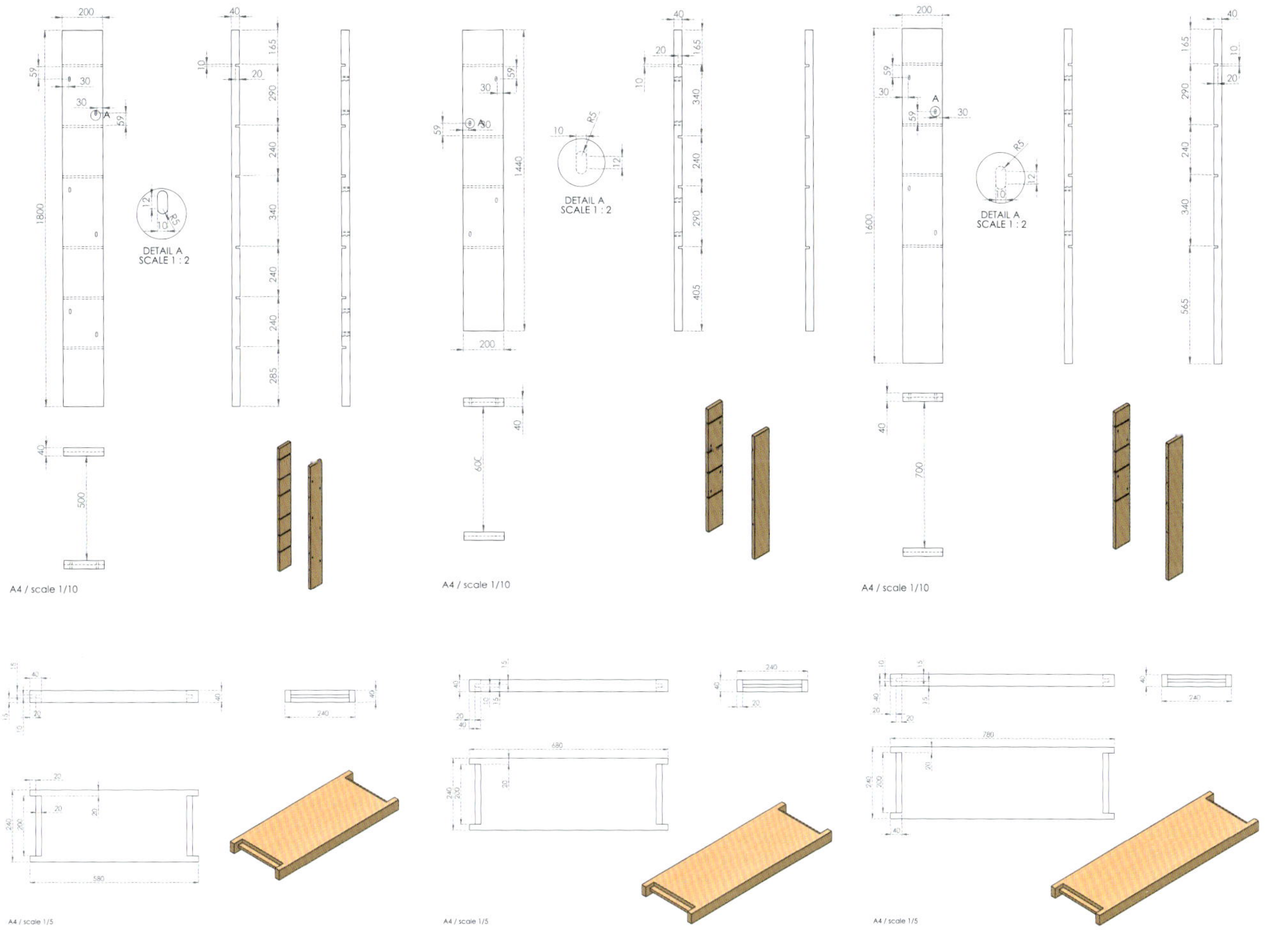

DETAIL A
SCALE 1 : 2

A4 / scale 1/10

DETAIL A
SCALE 1 : 2

A4 / scale 1/10

DETAIL A
SCALE 1 : 2

A4 / scale 1/10

A4 / scale 1/5

A4 / scale 1/5

A4 / scale 1/5

TUBERACK

» Joeri Reynaert
» Belgium

Tuberack is a shelf assembled without screws or glue—instead it is held together firmly by rubber tubes. The tubes form random patterns that can be used to display books or other items. Tuberack is made out of solid oak and comes in a flat figure, which is easy to assemble.

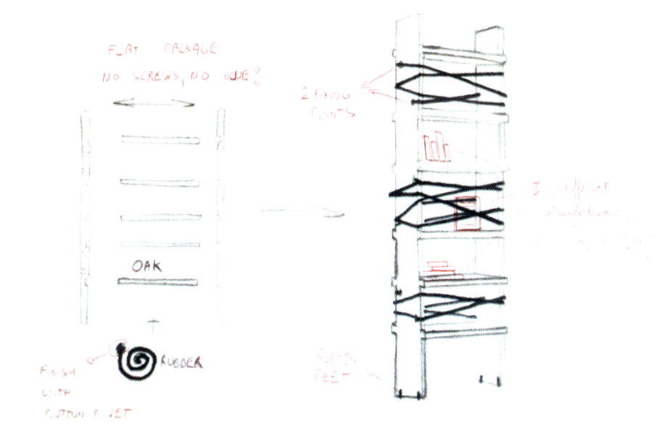

Terry Pratchett & Neil Gaiman
MÁLVERKIÐ
Silverstein
Where the Sidewalk Ends
THE SNOWBALL
ALICE SCHROEDER
WARREN BUFFETT
AND THE BUSINESS OF LIFE
ARNALDUR INDRIÐASON
TENDER MORSELS
THE BOOK OF LOST THINGS
The Book of Photography

BOOK RACK

» Gustav Johannsson, Agusta Magnusdottir / agustav
» Iceland

The Book Rack by agustav comes in solid oak, wenge and walnut. It's available in two sizes, using 6 or 12 pins/bookmarks depending on the size. The pins are detachable and can be moved around the back piece of book, to meet people's various needs. The designers have tested the racks and had book hanging for a while with no sign of wearing damage. The books are lined up on a small wooden plate so that the pages stay intact. The plates can be moved back and forth to control the height of which the book hangs, making it possible to line up books of different sizes in a straight line. The string is made of waxed cotton and is available in dark brown, beige or red.

ORBIT CABINET

» Kenyon Yeh
» Chinese Taipei

Made of MDF and tube steel painted in black or white the ORBIT cabinet enables a variety of combinations to suit the needs of the space. It can be detached in half to stand on the wall or to become two or three small cabinet. It is also stackable allowing transformation to different level of bookshelves.

HANG ON

› Tore Bleuzé, Nils Ferlin
› Belgium

Hang On is a bookshelf designed to be installed on slanted walls. It has a simple and basic design and can hold books A4 size and smaller. In addition, Hang On can be folded together for easy packaging and transport.

Photo ©Aaron Lapeirre

BOOK BOOKSHELF

› Rich & Harry
› UK

The Book Bookshelf was a project that came about after the designer saw a pile of left over books at the end of a jumble sale. The idea for a shelf made from books seems almost obvious, and the process from concept to completion was more of a refinement of function than of aesthetic intricacies.

ABACUS BOOKCASE

» Müge Sené, Cihangir Ünlütürk
» Turkey & France

Abacus Bookcase, as its name suggests, is inspired by the ancient calculation tool and brings a playful element to storing books. The bookcase is rather two dimensional and gains its third dimension when the books are placed on it. The user's interaction with the wooden beads adds playfulness to the design.

Photo ©Mustafa Nurdogdu

EFoS - ELASTIC FOLDING STRUCTURE

» Yuichi-ro Yamanaka / S.O.Y.LABO.
» Japan

Lattice, the simplest of materials connected by hinges of certain densities, creates function of elastic fold for this structure named EFoS. It was developed as a chair, a screen, a shelf and a lampshade. Wood latticework, one of the traditional elements of Japanese architecture, has a delicate relationship between light and shadow. By intersection of layers of lattices at various angles, EFoS obtains visual "moiré" effect and the "moiré" obtains spatial depth and complex aspects with movements of light and movements of the structure.

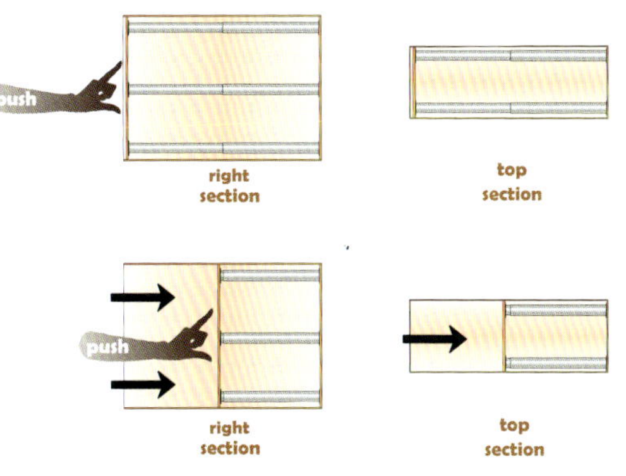

CLICK BOOKSHELF

» Tayyar Yildizoglu
» Turkey

This bookshelf is also a wall. When you push the shelf, it moves to the inside, leaving space for books. In this way, the wall turns into a bookshelf. Supported by chrome coated metal carriers, 18 mm and 25 mm MDF pieces are used in this design.

Photo ©Carolijn Slottje

FRAMES

› Gerard de Hoop
› The Netherlands

Frames is a bookcase that consists of five layers of plywood. The frames have different sizes and depths, so it is an appropriate place for books with various sizes. The cabinet can stand alone in the room.

FRAMES WALL

» Gerard de Hoop
» The Netherlands

Frames Wall is a wall-mounted cluster of squares and rectangles that provides space for books of various heights. The shelves pictured are made from lacquered black MDF, but they can also be made with other woods and in different sizes.

Amis
PARIS

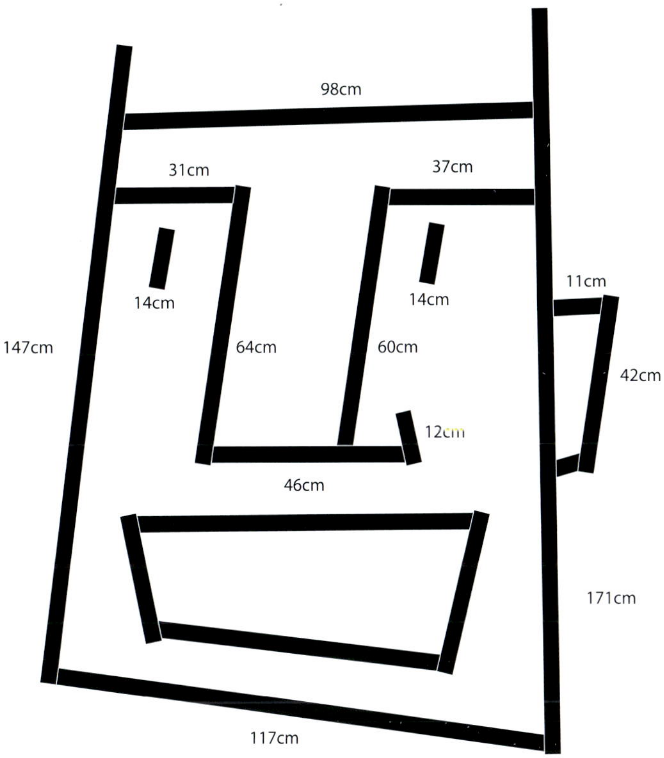

FACE SHELVING

» Alexi Mccarthy
» South Africa

The idea for this bookshelf originated from a conversation the designer had with his girlfriend who suggested that they could make interesting installations or even furniture out of his minimalistic drawing of faces. Exploring this project further the designer hoped that what people put on the shelf and their interaction with it would make a difference in the user's life.

FLOW I

› George Lee
› USA

Flow I came from the desire to create a design that features quality wood work at its most basic level. The thinly layered wood enables people to see its finest grains. By sanding thin pieces of maple plywood to create this effect, the natural wood are left exposed and thinly coated with polyurethane. Upon second look the piece seems to resemble a cargo ship when items are placed on it. This is an essential part of the piece with the designer's intention to stimulate and open up people's creativity. The more you add to the shelf and in particular ways the more it can resemble any particular cargo ship desired. This element of form and function is a trait common to the le mouton & co family.

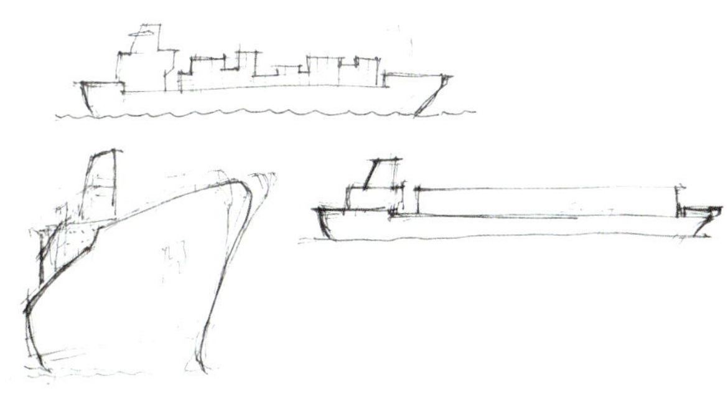

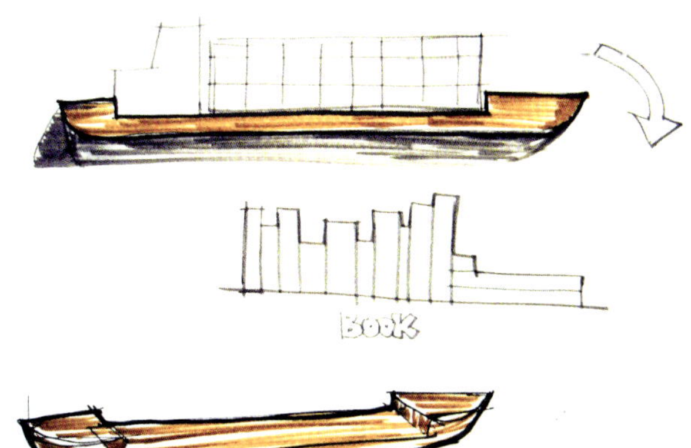
BOOK

FABRIC HINGE BOOKSHELVES

» Lisa Jo-Fan Chang
» Chinese Taipei

The use of plywood panels, leather and gravity in this project create a sturdy structure against any wall surface. The collapsible fabric hinges make transporting very easy and space saving, while the embedded magnets hold all the shelving panels together.

BLOCKSHELF

› Amy Hunting
› UK

Making use of blocks of wood and cotton rope as well as knots traditionally used for sailing and fishing, Blockshelf was created. You can pull the strings and the shelf will disassemble. It can easily be put together again. The material is collected from a local timber importer's waste bin in London and consists of over 20 types of wood. This is the first result of the rope and wood experiments. Using the beautiful wood waste mix that comes out of the massive wood floor industry, this shelf is recycled with pride. All shelves are unique and can easily be reconfigured by the user: they can be hung on the wall or from the ceiling, in which case they can also serve a room divider.

BOOKSHAPE

» Davide Radaelli
» Italy

Bookshape was first designed as a small freestanding design with a shape defined by an imaginary chaotic set of books, as the concept was that the content had to give shape to its container. It is made of acrylic poured in sheets, opal in color, on which two "double-sided" sheets, red or violet or green with a particular degree of pigment and transparency, are superimposed. The first and last sheets are "boxed" by polymerization which has the effect of making the sheets blend together, becoming a single body.

Tre camere a Manhattan
Simenon
131
Marte in Ariete
Lernet-Holenia
209
228
La pazienza dell'arrostito
Ceronetti
Il nostro ambiente cosmico
Rees
Durrell
Adelphi

Photo ©Alessandro Camilli

NEWTON

- Francesco Polare
- Italy

The Newton bookshelf is a clamp that rests on two hooks that have been screwed into the wall. It was created to suspend a reader's favorite books. Newton comes from the modification of an old clamp and holds the books to make a wall more interesting to look at.

Tolstoj
5
Goethe
19

ANITA

» Ricard Mollon / Quattria
» Spain

ANITA is an acrylic typographic thermoformed shelf. It is possible to customize any word you can imagine to hold books, picture frames, CDs, etc. This iconic piece of furniture is not only a shelf but also a room divider.

AAKKOSET SHELF / ROOM DIVIDER

» Lincoln Kayiwa
» Finland

The meticulous 4-week process to make just one AAKKOSET uniquely combines the very latest manufacturing technology with traditional local craftsmanship. In brief, handpicked cut-to-size number is fed through a 5-Axis Computer Numerically Controlled (CNC) router. It is thoroughly glued, pressed and primed before a deep rich paint job is first mechanically applied and then finished by hand. It is available in black, blue, green, orange, red, violet, yellow and white.

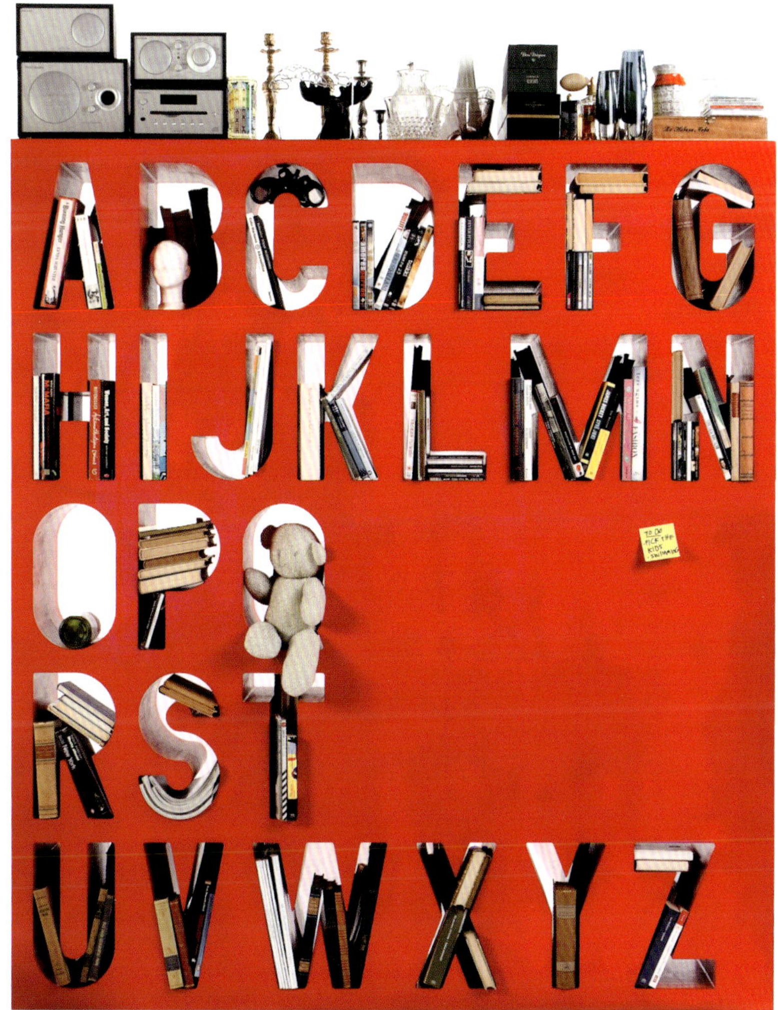

Photo ©John Dolci

GIVENS VITRINE

» Yogiaman Tracy Design
» USA

Measured samples of ornament were appropriated and digitally reformed to create this subtle intervention perched on either side of a monumental stair. Designed to blend into Givens Hall, a 1930's Beaux Arts building, the book vitrines are symmetrical in elevation and asymmetrical in plan. By squeezing one vertical edge closer to the wall the vitrines avoid direct light from adjacent windows and open to passing viewers. Custom steel brackets suspend books within a smooth, concave container. Without any perceptible edges the vitrine's internal, white surface visually flattens against the plaster walls, foregrounding front covers of the books.

KANTIK BOOKSHELF

» Patricia Yasmine Graf
» Germany

Kantik is a slightly slanted bookshelf made of a solid board, designed to lean against the wall. The simple design of this one-piece bookshelf makes it easy to be moved.

PRIMO QUARTO BOOKCASE

› Giuseppe Viganò
› Italy

This bookcase is arched like a waxing moon, which creates a strong decorative purpose. It consists of slanting internal shelves and dividers that create a curved line, with a decidedly harmonious effect.

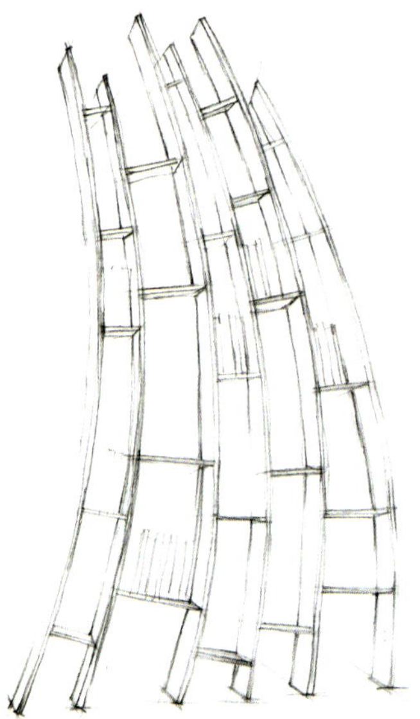

Photo ©Contratti Company

Photo ©James Champion

HOLDFAST

› Sam Weller
› UK

Holdfast began with the exploration of clamps and their infinite possibilities as both a tool and a joining device. The clamp elements that hold this range of furniture together are very simple in form. It is based on the holdfast clamping system typically used for holding material to the surface of a workbench. The components are manufactured using a computer-controlled wire-bending device. The components are then inserted into a through hole and wedged under the material they are supporting, creating tension in the vertical leg and in turn creating a strong stiff supporting structure for shelves as well as side tables, stools and other occasional home furnishings.

Frank Lloyd Wright's Usonian Houses
WRIGHT
IN THE DESIGN OF BUILDINGS
SCANDINAVIAN FURNITURE
COROT
brand-new
Before Mickey
Crafton
William Dyce

CANTO CORNER

» Andre Pereira
» UK

Canto Corner shelving units make use of dead corner spaces to accommodate books of varying depths and sizes. By utilizing the corner's angle and by placing deeper books towards the middle of the units, the Canto Corner utilizes the dead corner space efficiently without having books protruding from the shelf. When multiple units are mounted, the negative space in between provides extra book storage, and due to the offset shelves and powder coated metal, the books have something to lean on preventing them from toppling over. The flat pack units are made from CNC routed 15mm plywood board with an American white oak veneer on one side and white high-pressure laminate on the opposite. Because of the way it was designed, it can be easily assembled with only a 4mm hexagonal key.

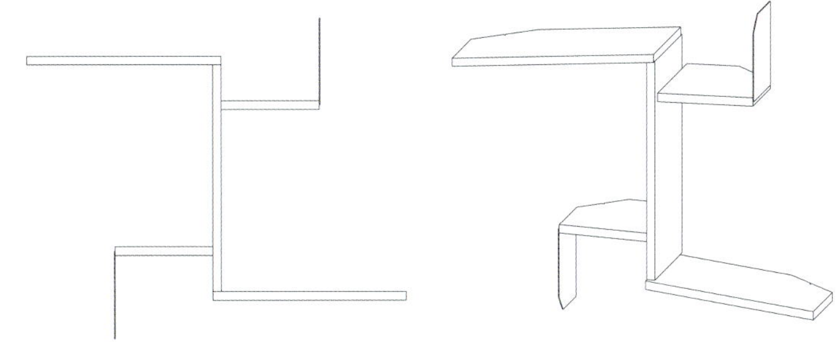

BOOK XSHELF

» Tarik Ali Sert, Tayfun Bilgin, Lokman Demirer
» Germany

Book XShelf is a project that creates flexible shelves for various sizes of books. This idea sprang from scissor lifts for adjustable platforms.

LAICA BOOKSHELF

▸ Francesco Innocenti / Officina11 Studio
▸ Italy

The idea of a compromise between changing and unchanging, between movement and preservation sparked the design of this bookshelf in a different, unusual way with a different use and interpretation. The bookshelf was produced in a limited collection of six pieces in different colors and finishes. In this process, each piece encapsulates the original sculpture's inspiration while adding the charm of art. The frame is made of resin, reinforced with fiberglass to ensure extra mechanic resistance and flexibility.

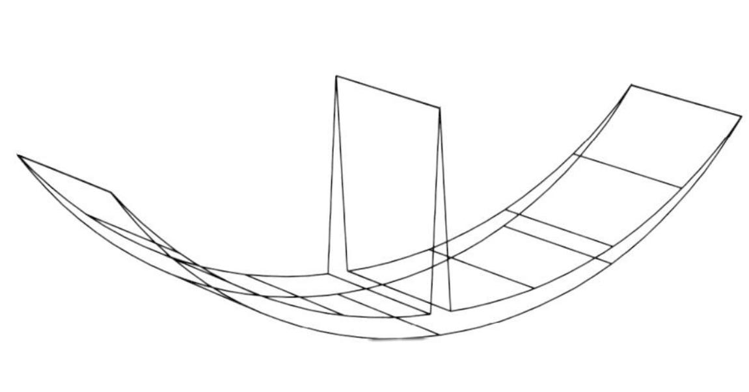

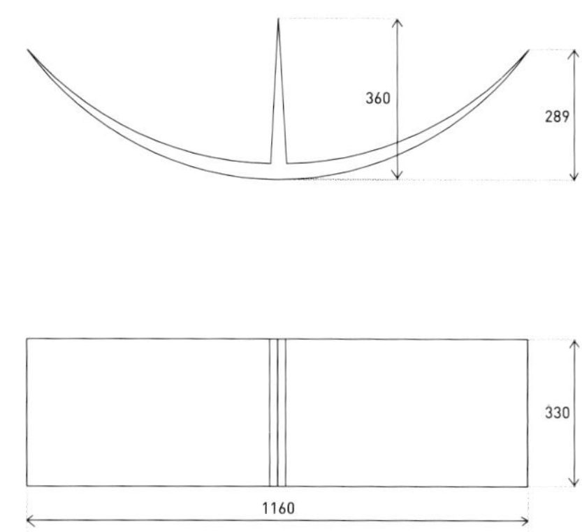
360
289
330
1160

Photo ©Kęstutis Kurienius

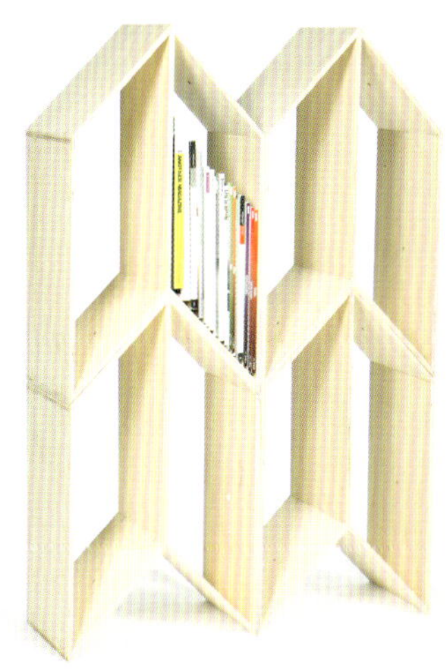

WEAVES/AUDŽIU

» Rapolas Gražys
» Lithuania

The design was inspired by classic ornaments of the ethnic Lithuanian culture. "Weaves / Audžiu" is a system of modular shelving made of plywood, which, starting from a basic and essential element is capable of providing various options, from simple shelving to displayer, from magazine holder to book shelf. The multi-functional geometric segment leaves the user free to "weave" a unique composition by assembling and customizing multiple units according to various needs and desired aesthetic result.

RACCONTO PLURALE

• Sara Bergando
• Italy

The round shape of the Racconto Plurale bookshelf connotes metaphorically culture continuity. The bookshelf maintains a flexible and widely customizable structure. Starting from the original C configuration, the modular structure allows different options and various combinations. Two materials, wood and iron, symbolize two alternatives: emotional/analog books, rational/digital multimedia. Raw materials and surface processing are environmentally friendly and respect the idea: Design for Disassembly.

Goethe

NEW YORK

TESSELLATION BOOKSHELF

• Jorge Javier Cruz Florin
• Mexico

Located in the entrance of a gallery, the concept of the bookshelf was to make a contrast between the colonial architecture of the place and contemporary art. Inspired by the geometric tessellations and possibilities in the field of design, the designer came up with the idea of a modular bookshelf that allows different types of arrangements. Using triangular shapes around quadrilateral shapes fixed on the wall, all the pieces are joined together by simple nut and bolt assembly so it can be arranged in many possibilities by adding or removing joints. There are four kinds of shapes, with different lengths and four colors: black, light grey, dark grey and white. When combined together, they create a three-dimensional look.

Photo ©Dante Busquets

SAP

» Ian Ortega
» Mexico

SAP shelves are manufactured in three different models, which can be installed individually or in groups in different combinations. Because of their shapes and hanging system, each shelf can be assigned a different function and can be installed with different orientations. In addition to the flat surface where objects may be rested, SAP number 1 also has a series of sections that extend to either side for coat hangers.

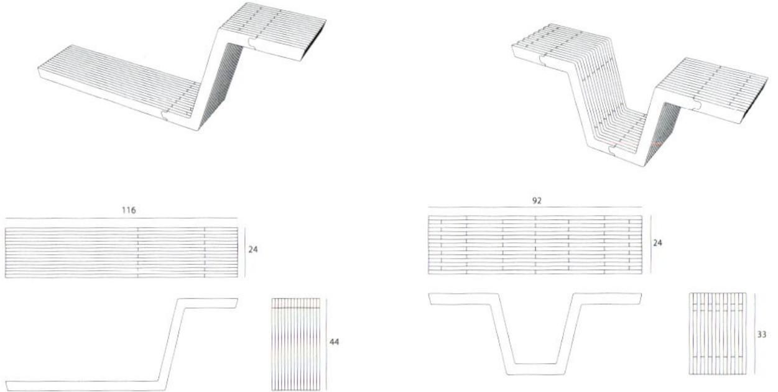

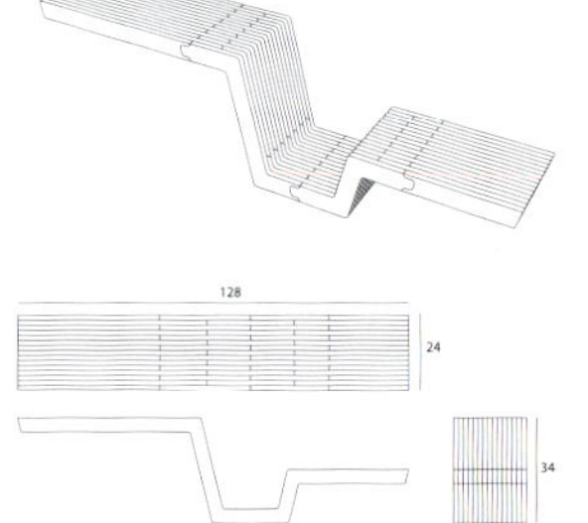

MAGDA

» Jordi Pedemonte, Eric Castelló, Jon Azkoitia / Artik Project
» Spain

MAGDA is a minimalist bookshelf in which books are supported by three points, both arms and the wall. Its installation does not require a level because the bookshelf works while any of its arms is above the horizontal axis. Users can let fly their imagination by creating multiple compositions.

Photo ©Karin Demeyer

C74L49

» Erick Demeyer, Steven Leprize
» France

The design is created by adding unexpected bends between two identical surfaces. These elements are used in adjustable systems and can be used to compose different types of furniture. Acrylic stone panels are added to the wood in order to create the functional surface.

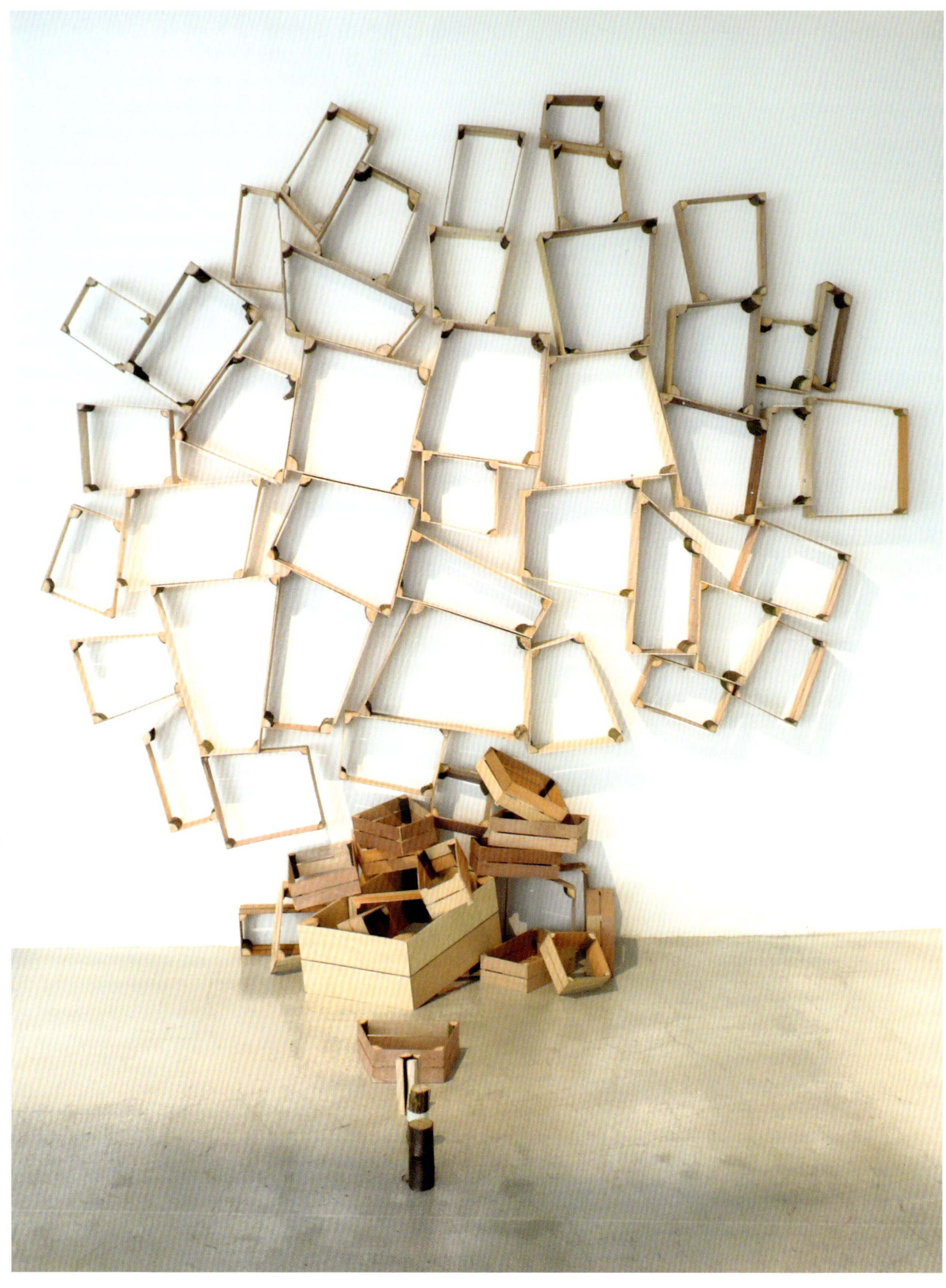

SPLIT

» Peter Marigold
» UK

Each Split Box is created from a single log split into four unequal pieces. The resulting box is irregular but always perfectly complete because the combined angles total 360 degrees. The outcome is chaotic yet has its own system.

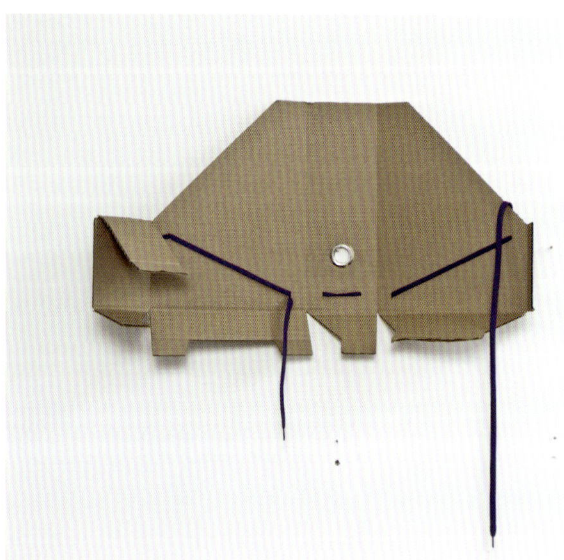

NN BOOKSHELF

• Wenchuman
• Chile

NN is a bookshelf made out of classical cardboard, hanging on a wall by itself. Borrowing the structure from an unknown author, it simplifies the bookshelf to its minimum, allowing the user the maximum amount of liberty to add, multiply and extract as needed. To hold more weight a lace design fits around the outside of the shell strengthening the weakest points. It reflects the quote by Dieter Rams: "Good design is invisible."

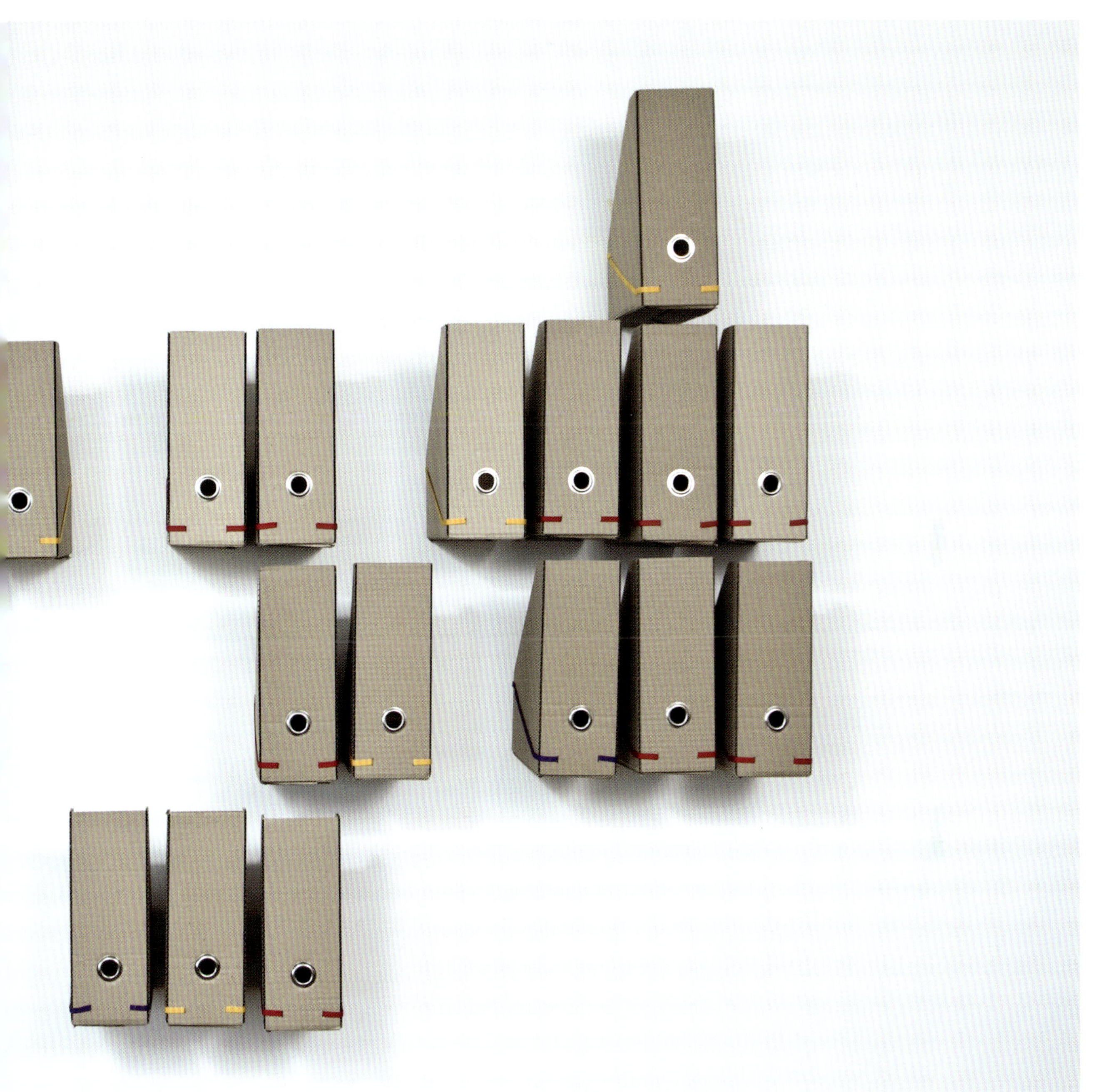

Photo ©BeaMalevich
THE BODY
LOFTS
Minimalismo
Box 1-7
by Pekka Kuivamäki
BeaMalevich
art and creativity
beamalevich.com
Box 1-7

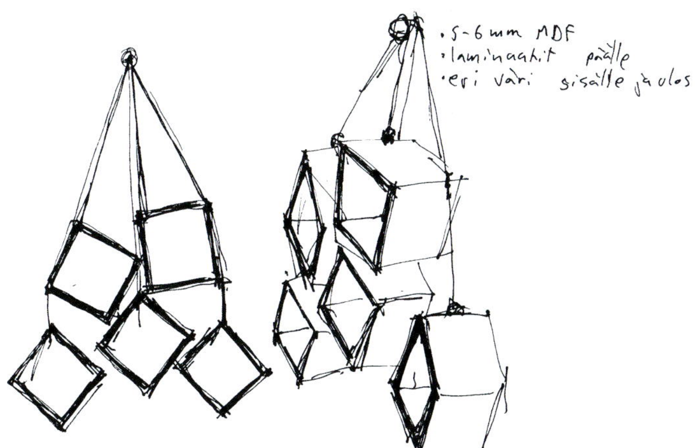

BOX 1-7

» Pekka Kuivamäki
» Finland

Box 1-7 is a modular shelf made of seven identical boxes of different sizes. As a hanging shelf, the different sizes of the boxes and the different lengths of the ropes offer countless ways to arrange and rearrange Box 1-7 on the wall. According to Pekka Kuivamäki, the inspiration for Box 1-7 came from a variety of artists and movements, including the suprematism of Kazimir Malevich, the neoplasticism of Piet Mondrian, the minimalism of Donald Judd and various other movements.

Photo ©Mcnair Evans

THE FIN COLLECTION

› Michael Metiu
› USA

The design objective was to create a piece of art that served as a function for displaying and storing books and collectibles. Designer also wanted the piece to be open to interpretation by the owner, which was achieved by designing the shelves so they can be mounted in a variety of ways, vertical, horizontal, or at a diagonal angle. The large shelf can even be freestanding on the floor or laid across a dresser. The construction is all hand made in Brooklyn and involves bent glue laminated plywood, with hidden fasteners, creating an incredibly lightweight and strong shelf that gives the illusion of shelf floating on the wall.

Photo ©Murat Seyman

TARGETBOOKS SHELF

- Mebrure Oral
- Turkey

The TarGetBooks Shelf is a bookshelf that helps organize books into two simple categories and bookcase: "read" and "will be read". When people buy a new book and plan to read it later, after a short time it gets forgotten in the "organized" chaos that bookcases create. The aim of the design of TarGetBooks is based on this. This special shelf is basically designed for separating the books that reader has read and will read. It shows people their target books all the time. The user can just buy books, put them on the shelf and never forget or postpone the reading plans. It stimulates people, attracts their attention and encourages them to read more.

WILL BE READ...
BUY·OLOGY
Steve Jobs

Photo ©Patrick Gries, Studio RS

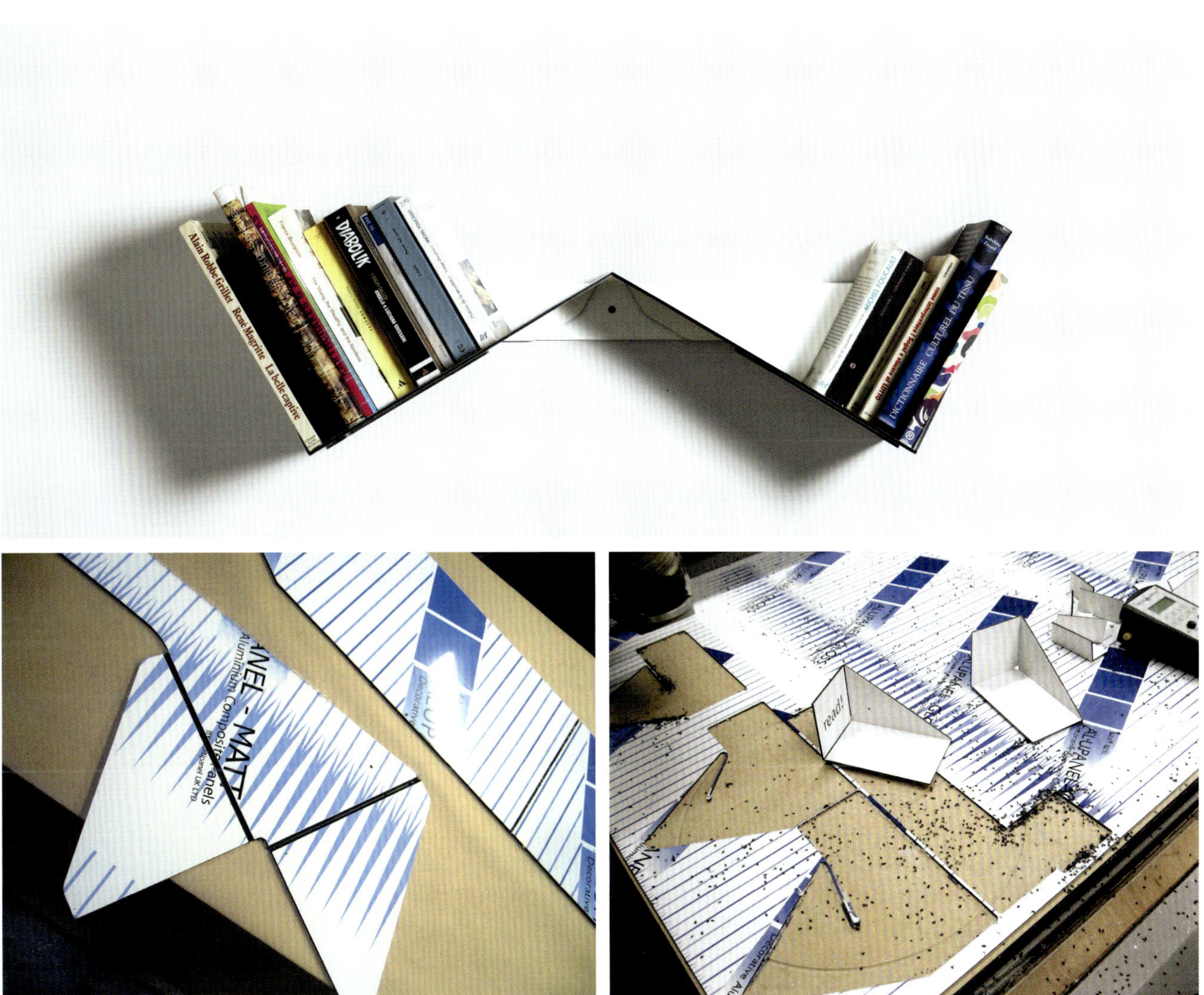

TRANSITORY BOOKSHELF

› Robert Stadler
› France

The Transitory Bookshelf combines two inclined platforms. The "read!" section reminds the reader to take time to read, while the "read." section's purpose is to help digest the books that have recently been read before they disappear into the jungle of your main bookshelf.

SERPENT

» Bashko Trybek
» Poland

This modular shelving system consists of four zigzagging wires and four wooden planks. The adjustable structure allows users to choose desired dimensions of the shelf in different spaces.

QUARTER CASE

- Ward Huting
- The Netherlands

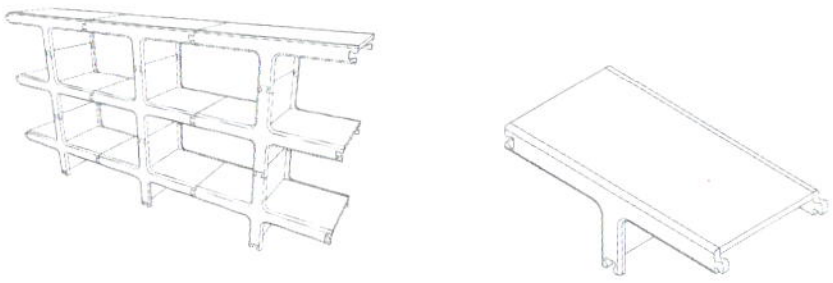

Quarter Case consists of modular cross-shaped elements, which can be fitted onto each other. In this way a case can be constructed in accordance with specific individual wishes, which can easily be enlarged in a variety of ways and directions. Quarter Case can be freestanding so that the shelves are accessible from both sides. The size of the shelves is based on the A4 file system, which renders Quarter Case ideal for the office.

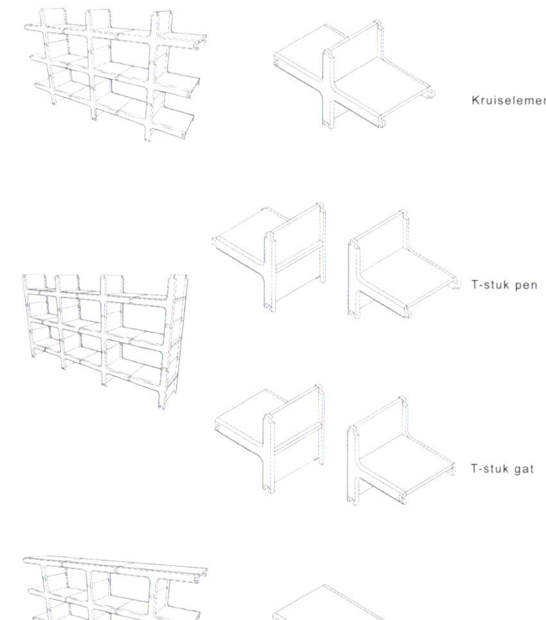

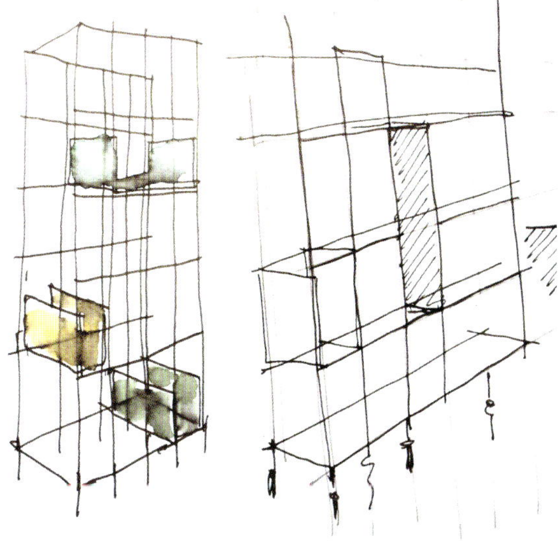

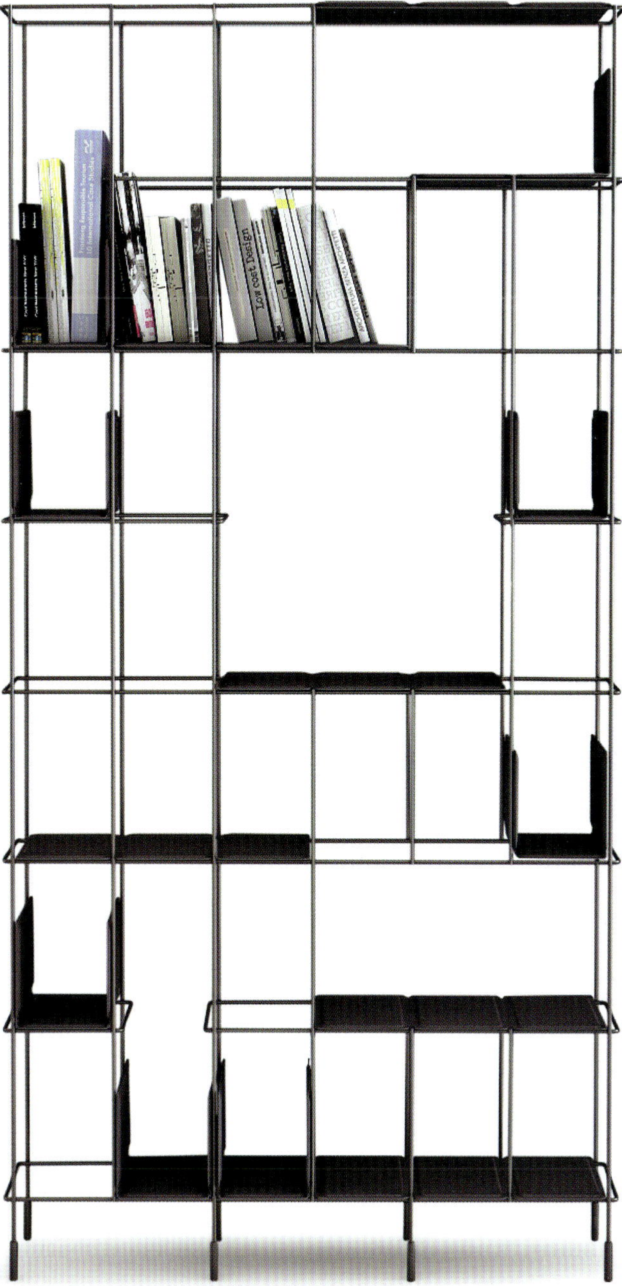

NETWORK

» Eva Paster, Michael Geldmacher
» Germany

This light modular bookcase features a slender structure and floating panels. These panels, made of leatherette, change the configuration of the bookcase in line with the metallic structure, allowing a total customization of the composition. In this way it creates a game of spaces between shelves, inviting users to combine and change the design at any moment.

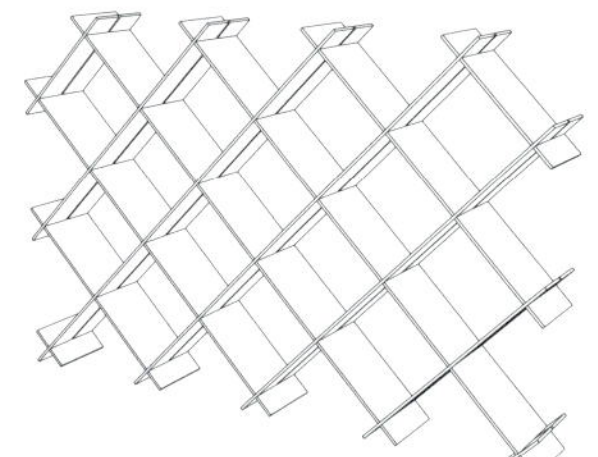

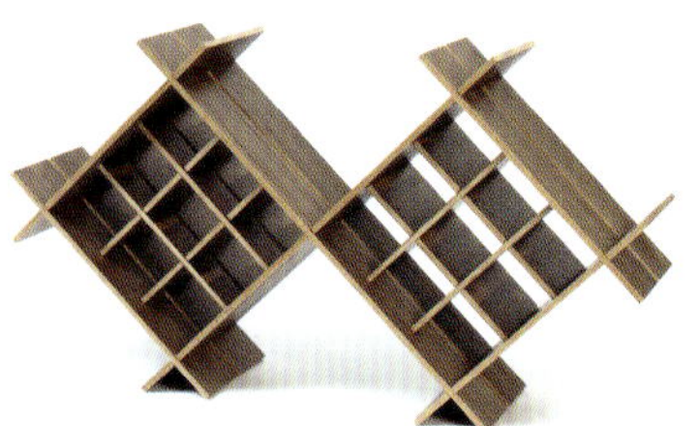

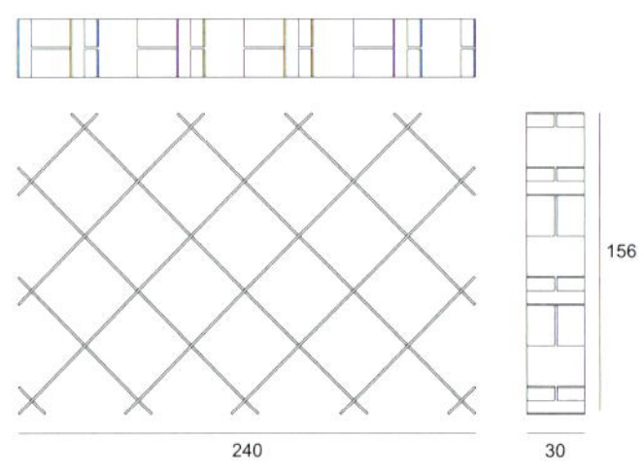

X BOOKSHELF

» Alejandro Castro
» Mexico

These shelves belong to a series of "X" bookshelves. The small size racks can be used for wine storage, while large size racks can be bookshelves. The module fits perfectly within the shelves, and users may utilize multiple spaces depending on the size of their collection.

Photo ©Cortesia Pirwi

INVERSO

› Studio Jens Praet
› Italy

Inverso is a storage system composed of marble blocks and particle board shelves. The wooden particle gain is turned into an elegant glossy material and like laminated furniture. Any superfluous marks made during assembly are removed, turning this material into aesthetically refined shelves. The marble blocks are produced with modern production techniques transforming this archaic material into contemporary objects.

CUBOS

» Emiliano Godoy, Juan Zouain
» Mexico

This modular bookcase is a very versatile storage form for books and other objects of various sizes. Six different modules are available. The height of three small ones stacked one on top of the other is the same as two large ones, which permits the creation of flat surfaces and empty spaces. The Cubos may be placed on the floor, over a desk or credenza, or on the top of the base of the same set.

Photo ©Enrique Macias

Industrial Design A-Z
Restroom
Diseño de productos
product design
Product Design
ICONS OF DESIGN
Light
100 DISEÑOS 100 AÑOS
Sport Design
Recuerdos de Chocolate
1000 chairs
1000 LIGHTS
EL DISEÑO
TASCHEN

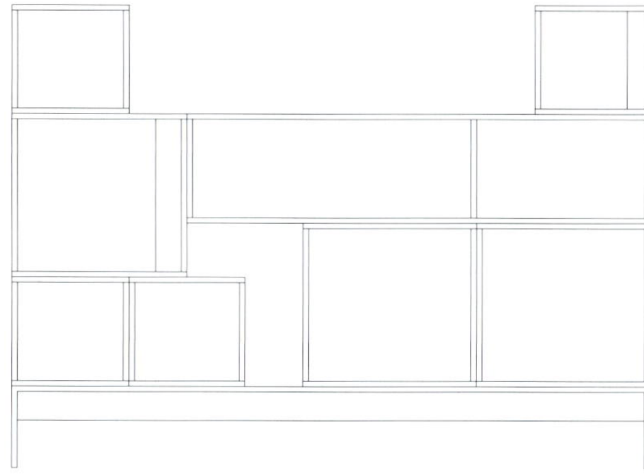

LONDON
Story of O
Pauline Reage
THE REVOLUTION OF EVERYDAY LIFE
RAOUL VANEIGEM
Modoc
RALPH HELFER
TALKING ART 1
WORDS IN PLACE
Paul Matthews
Flightless

KENN

BRIA

KENN BRONZE

» Kenyon Yeh
» Chinese Taipei

To connect the body and the leg part of these bookshelves, the designers used no screws but bronze cast resin. The body was made from pine stained with mahogany colour. The result is whimsical and attractive in addition to its practical use. Each shelf has multiple roles, accommodating items such as books, magazines, crafts, picture frames, etc. Items can be placed horizontally or at an angle.

Photo ©Studio Badini

ASSEMBLAGE

» Seletti
» Italy

This modular bookshelf is made in lacquered MDF. The cubes can be combined in different ways to meet different needs. It takes up very little space as they can be placed one inside another like Russian dolls.

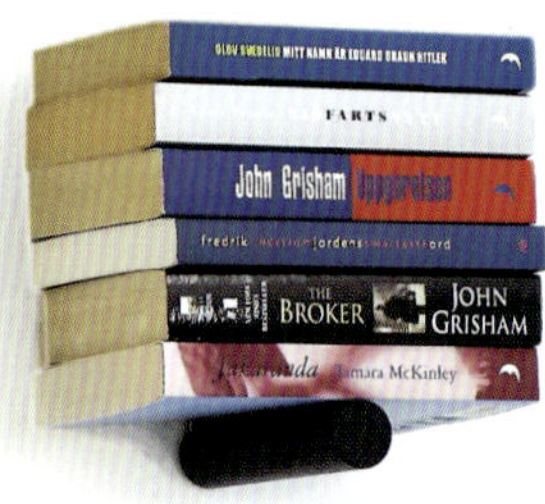

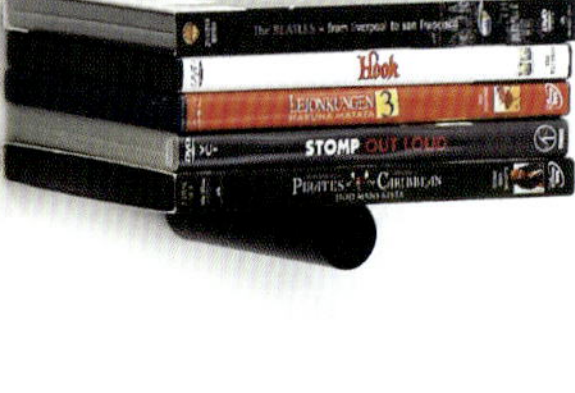

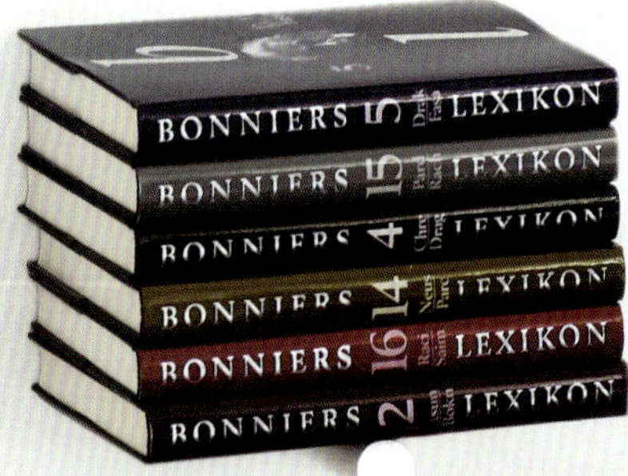

Photo ©Jonas Sällberg

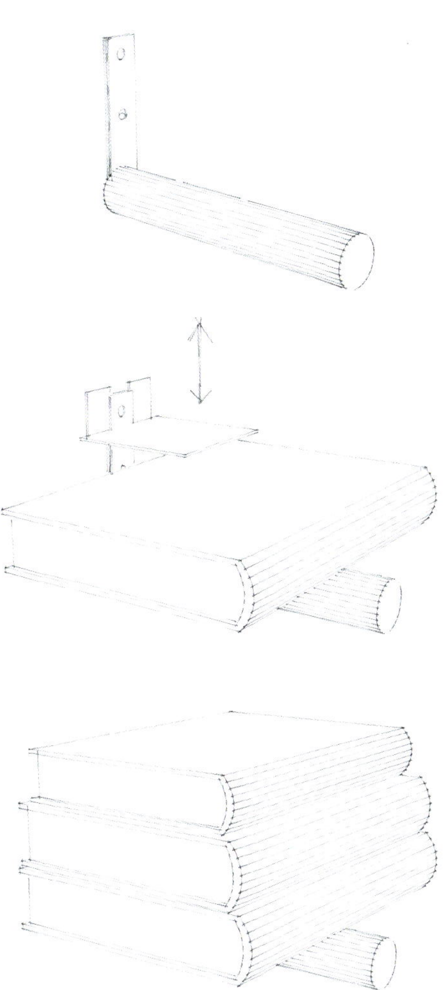

BOOKSHELF PINIWINI

» Linus Svärm
» Sweden

Piniwini is a small wall-mounted peg that works like a shelf. When books, CDs and DVDs are stacked on the shelf, they appear to be perfectly balanced on the top of the peg. The idea to this shelf was born when the designer was a student living in a very cramped dorm. The purpose of this bookshelf, apart from having a small footprint, is to put a smile on people's faces.

Photo ©Curzio Catelan

WWW

» Viktor Matic
» Italy

As a shelf with a digital angle, this project is titled simply: "www". The surface of this object dissolves into strings, which connect and transform into other new surfaces. The shelf is an interpretation of the archetype of a shelf. Between form and function, between space and dimension, between a "not-yet" and "not-anymore", it creates concrete opportunities and specific associations. Through its parts, it is not only a modular system, but also a type of installation in an ever-changing space.

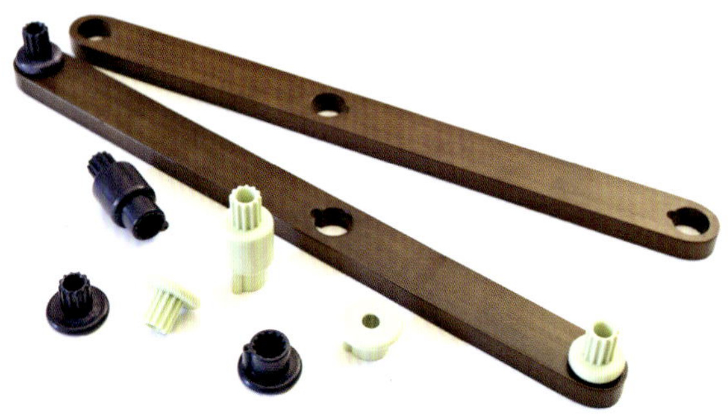

BAMBICA

» Andrew Gancikov, John Fitzpatrick
» Lithuania

Bambica is a creative modern furniture using bamboo and other sustainable materials. It can be constructed in different forms and be disassembled easily. The flat-pack design allows for efficient and low-cost transportation of the product. The product stands for individual creativity, modular concept, functionalism and durability.

Photo ©Maja Galli

La Società Umanitaria Fondazione P. M. Loria Milano
LA GUERRA A COLLECCHIO
Wassily Kandinsky

THE STORY BEHIND

My partner John Fitzpatrick stayed in Hong Kong for a period of time. He was fascinated by the bamboo scaffolding used in building skyscrapers. It is such a strong, light and plentiful material. We thought of bamboo which is a local material in China with intrinsic structural and iconic qualities. But typical "Bali style" bamboo furniture was not what we wanted. We intended to develop a bamboo design which is more like the 21st century. Its flexibility reflects the notion that everyone could be an artist, and satisfies the end user's desire for participation and self-expression. In fact, Bambica has its roots in modular furniture design which has been around since the 1930's. What we have done was taking the modular bookshelf one step further—hand over the design direction to the customer. That is why we have reduced the design to "sticks and stones".

D.I.Y.

As the bookshelf is an extremely important item in domestic environment and it holds the books that form part of your thoughts, we value the idea of being able to shape our own bookshelf, in other words, to reflect our personalities not only through the books on the rack. It holds your books, the words of which form part of your thoughts. You can shape your own bookshelf to reflect your personality by changing the shape of the shelf itself or the books on it.

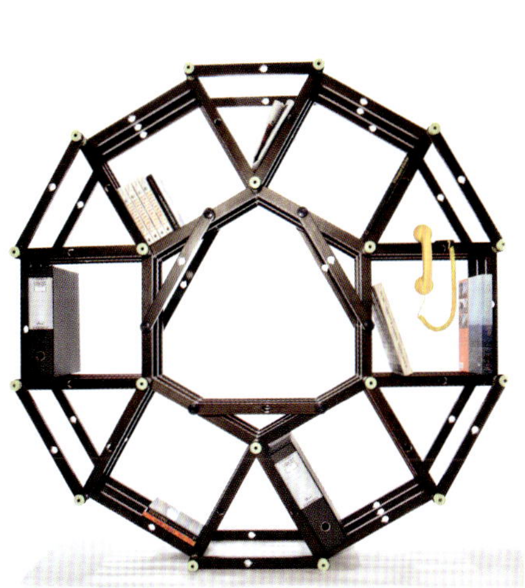

ELASTIC SHELF

› Helbert Suarez Ferreira, Remi Melander
› Spain

This practical and adaptable shelf system for home or office supported by two used furniture legs is made of bicycle tires. It creates an interesting elastic structure that can be used to store and manage books as well as other objects. The use of recycled tires provides not only a way to reuse discarded material but a new look to the room.

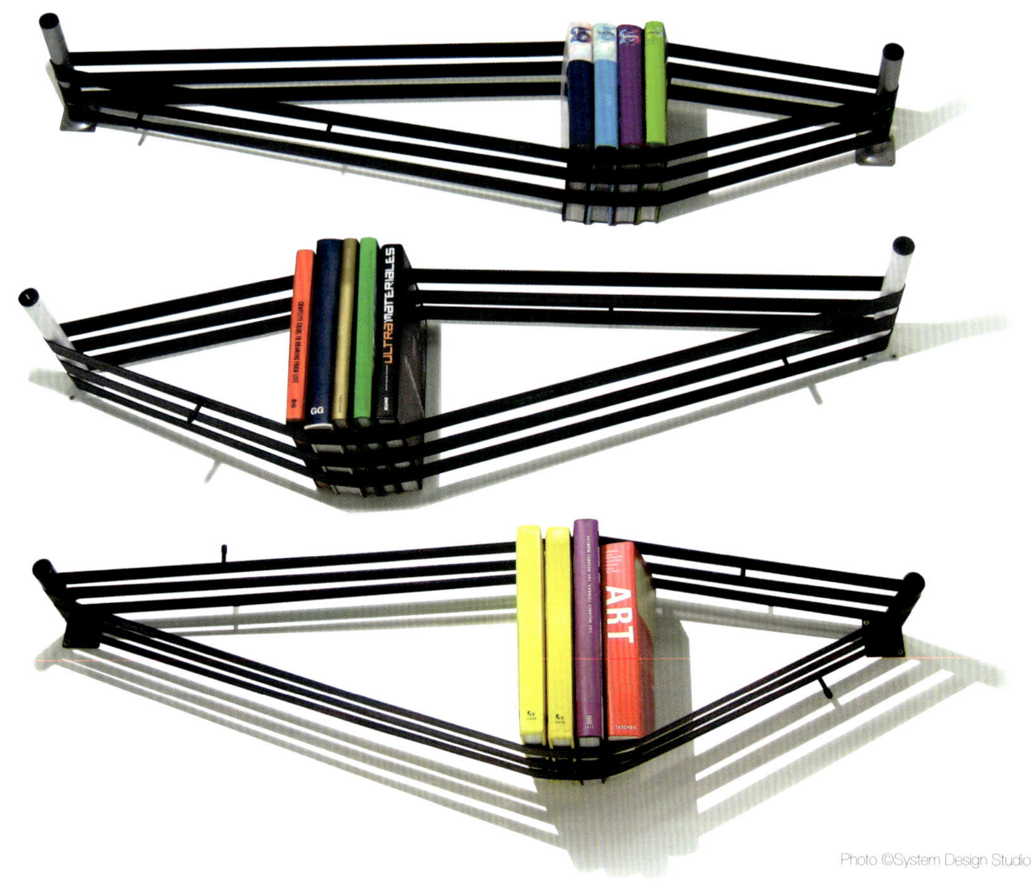

Photo ©System Design Studio

FA.B.

» Aliki Rovithi, Foant Asour
» Greece

The Fa.B. fabric bookcase is an eco-focused book storage system with a minimal environmental impact and a new way to arrange and protect books and magazines. It is suitable for homes and offices, and can be used as a bookcase and a room divider at the same time. "Fa.B." offers users a renewable storage space: it is made of birch plywood, and the fabric units are made of a recyclable, resilient, stain resistant, wrinkle-free fabric. The use of the durable fabric along with the minimum amount of wood, allows users to consume as little natural resources and raw materials as possible. The piece is a foldable, easy to assemble and flat-pack furniture. The self-assembly feature helps to reduce volume and stay environmentally friendly during transportation.

Photo ©Diana Balogh-Tyszko

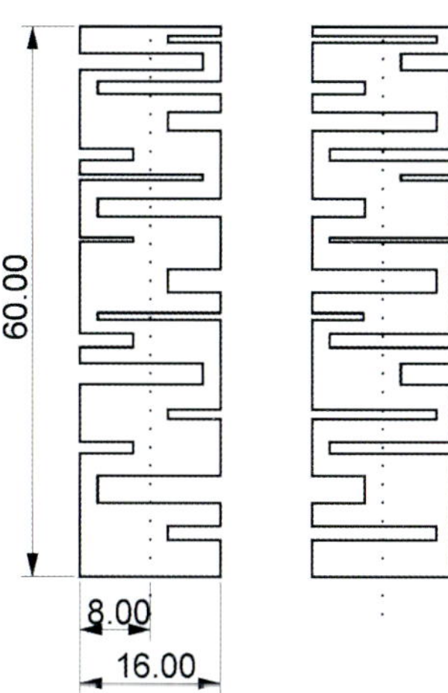

BOOK SHELF

• Rick Ivey
• Canada

This piece is a re-examination of the typical bookshelf, inspired by the challenge to store art books that vary widely in size and shape. The designer intended to transform the static orientation of the typical bookshelf into a project that allows the books to become something more. By storing the books horizontally, the spines become easier to read and more accessible rather than simply stored. The intention with this product was to create an ideal product for both open-concept spaces and small condos. With a column configuration, the books can be accessed from all sides while taking up minimal floor space.

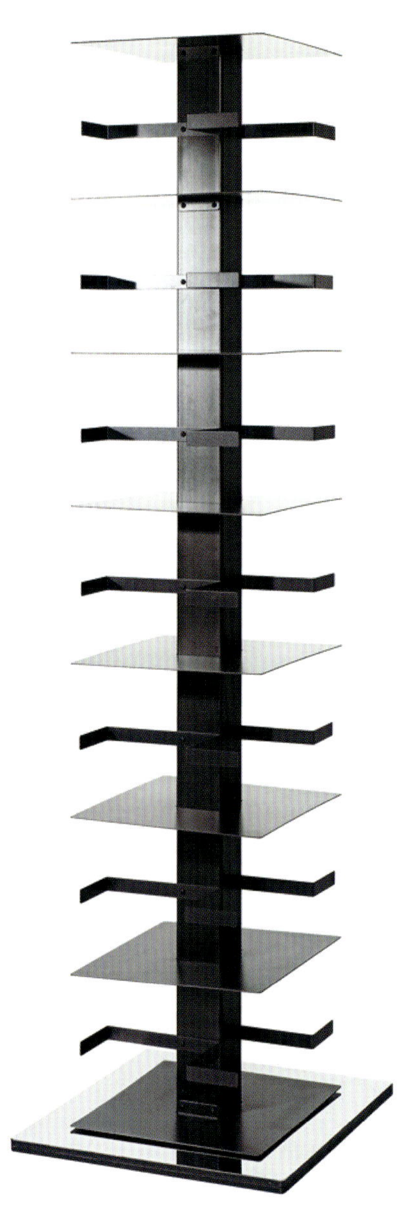

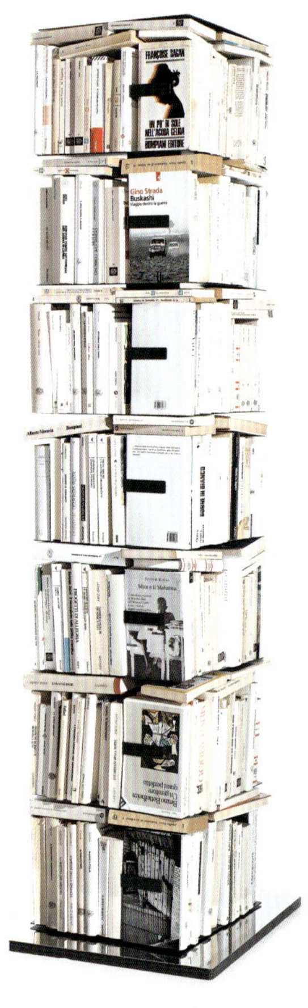

PTOLOMEO X4

» Bruno Rainaldi
» Italy

Vertical and freestanding, Ptolomeo is a three-dimensional revolving bookcase. Its structure and shelves are available in black metal or white lacquered polished steel. Ptolomeo transforms jumbles of books into an interesting interior decoration.

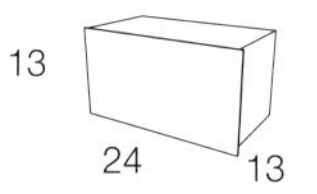

OBJECT HOLDER

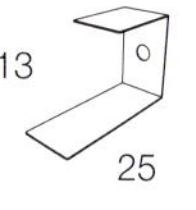

EXTENSION

2
1

CD HOLDER

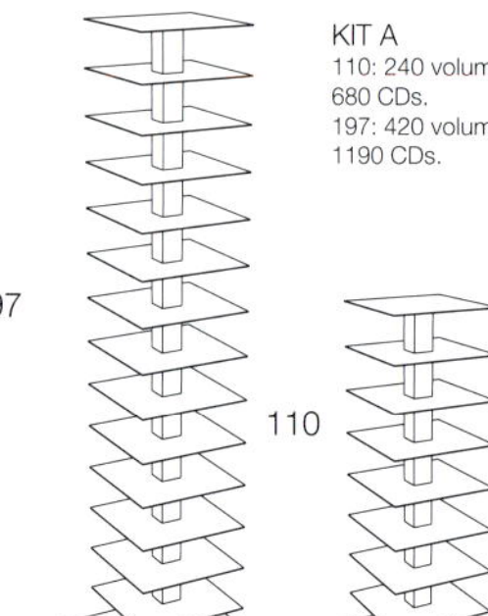

KIT A
110: 240 volumes or 680 CDs.
197: 420 volumes or 1190 CDs.

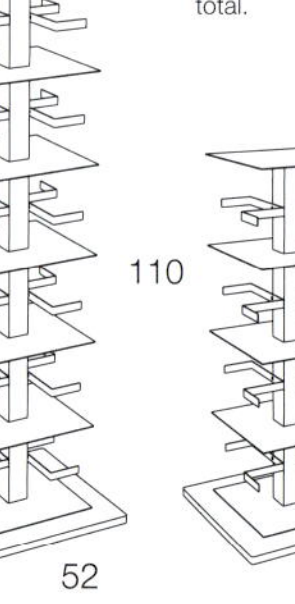

110
52

KIT B
110: 140 volumes total volumes or 680 CDs.
197: 245 volumes total.

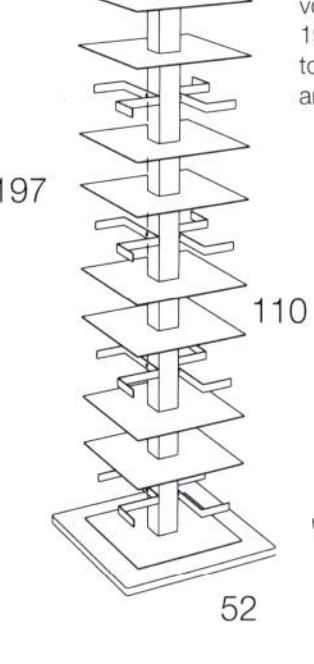

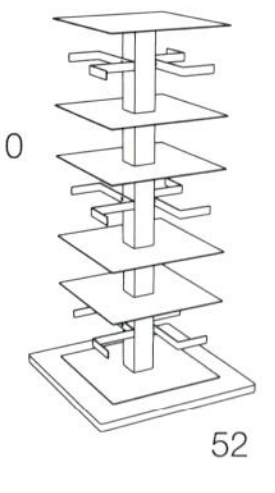

KIT C
110: 165 volumes total volumes or 105 volumes and 170 CDs.
197: 295 volumes total or 175 volumes and 340 CDs.

Photo ©Ezio Manciucca

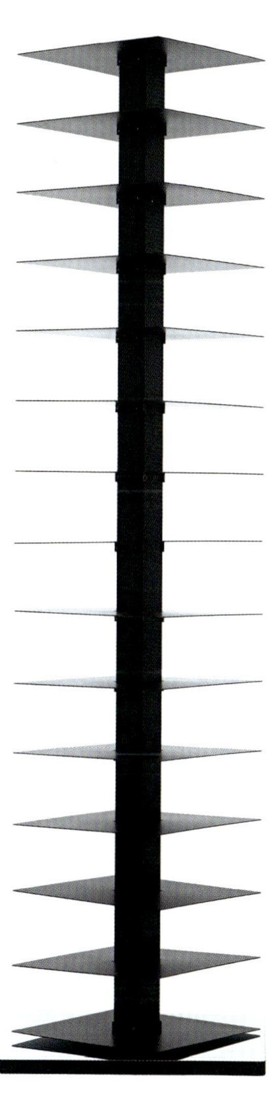

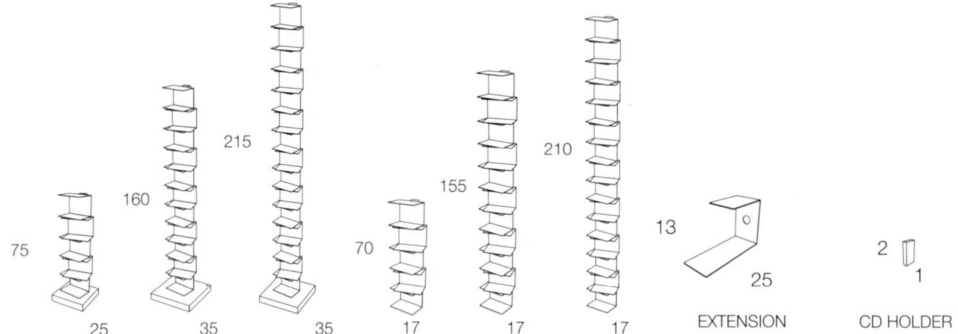

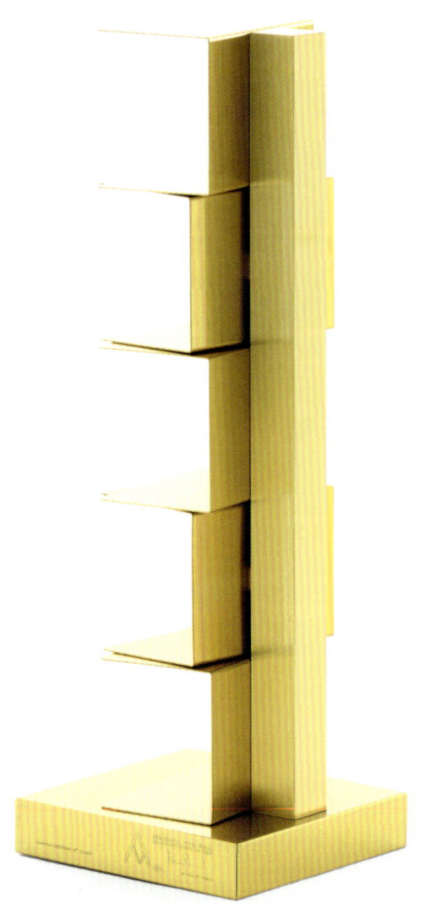

ORIGINAL PTOLOMEO

- Bruno Rainaldi
- Italy

This vertical self-standing bookcase, engraved with the designer's signature on the base, is finely finished off: Structure and shelves in black metal, polished stainless steel (the inside of the shelves in satin finish), white RAL 9016 metal, raw metal with transparent protective finish. Base in polished stainless steel, black RAL 9011 metal, white RAL 9016 metal, raw metal with transparent protective finish. In addition, there is extension in metal lacquered black or white as well as a magnet cd holder.

Photo ©Ezio Manciucca

INTERNI
Ottagono
FRAME 47 NOV/DEC 2005 STAGE SETS HOTELS SHOPS EDUCATION AND HEALTHCARE
FRAME 45 JUL/AUG 2005 MILAN EDUCATION THEATRE OFFICES AND PUBLIC SPACES
FRAME 41 NOV/DEC 2004 FASHION SHOPS HOUSES EXHIBITION STUDENTS DISPLAY

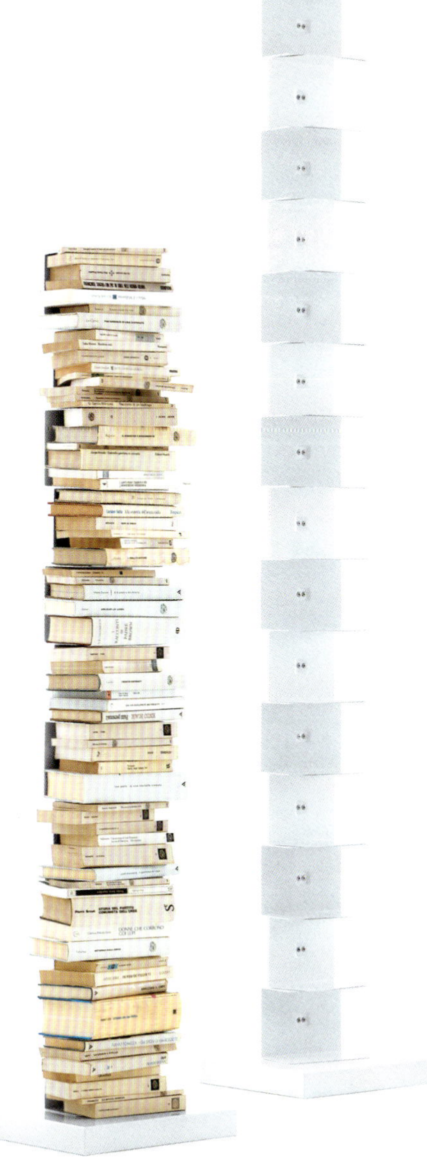

UPTOWN

- Lapo Ciatti
- Italy

Uptown is a bookshelf made up of vertical containers. It is available in four different heights with a lacquered distribution frame and solvent-free anti-scratch paint. The fixed shelves can store books, CDs, DVDs, etc. depending on the user's needs. It is provided with a double wall fitting as well.

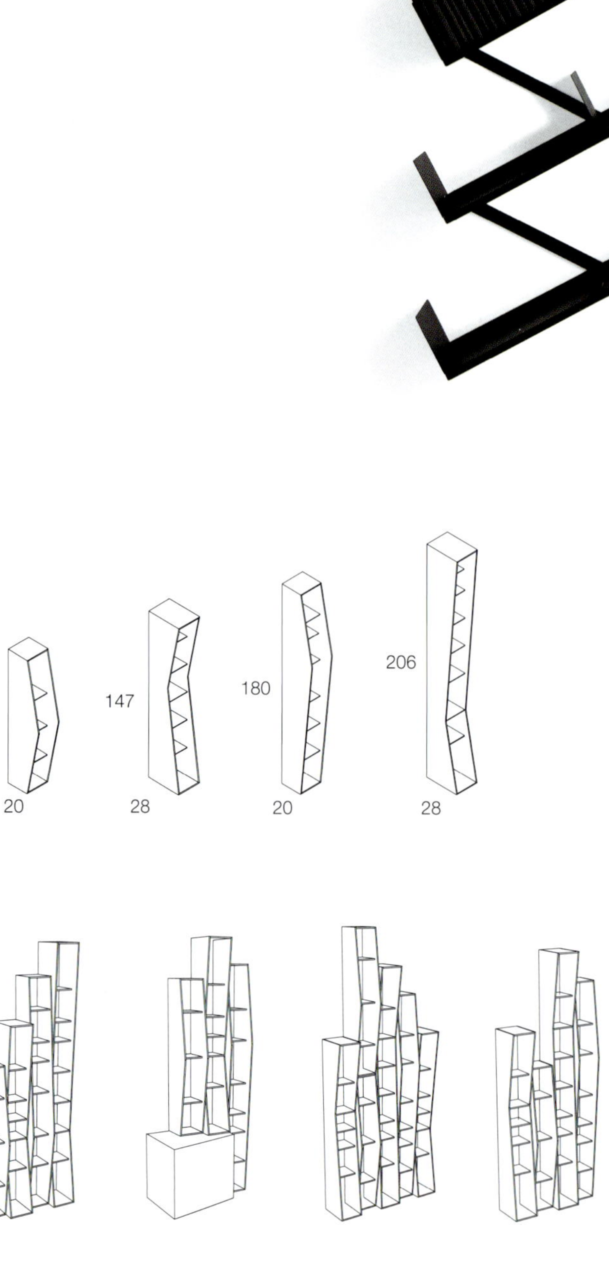

Photo ©Ezio Manciucca

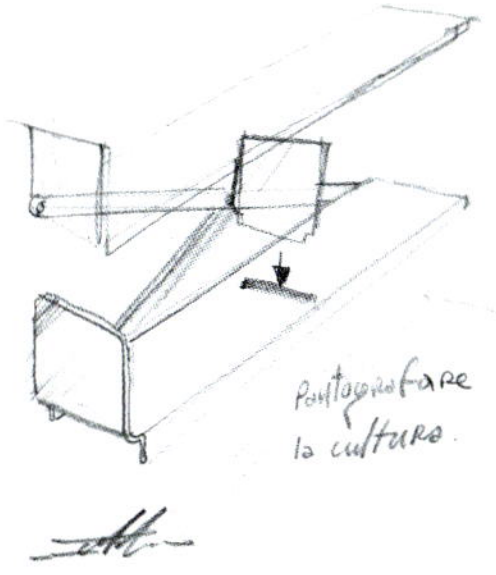

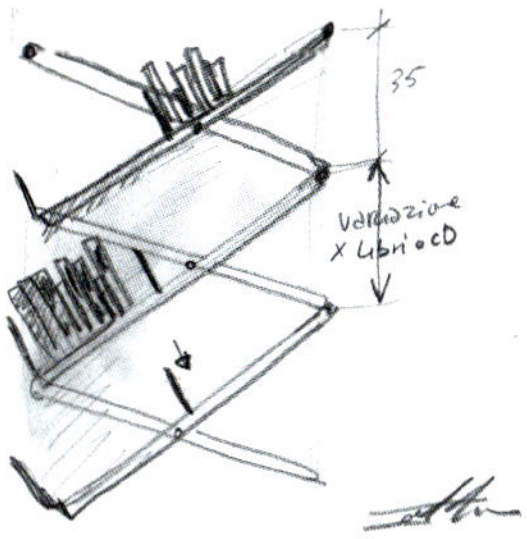

BOOXX + MINIBOOXX

» Denis Santachiara
» Italy

The double X figure of this design allows a free bookcase position on the wall, to satisfy either aesthetics or space requirements. The bookcase comes with steel plate frame and sheet metal shelves and has removable bookends in metal sheet. Galvanized zinc (only Booxx), matt white and matt black lacquered are the main materials.

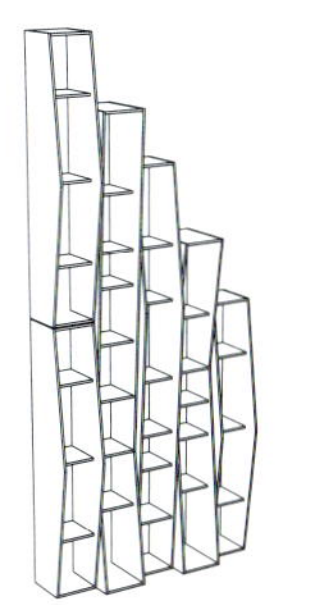

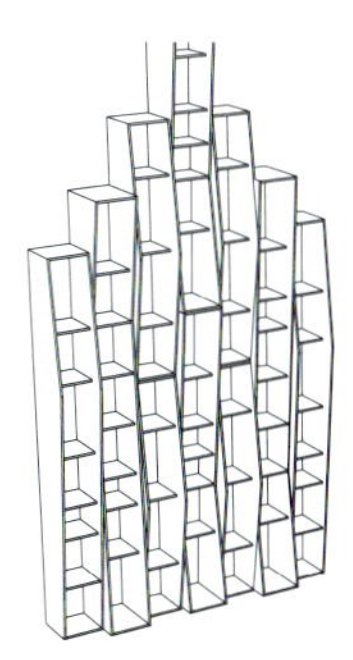

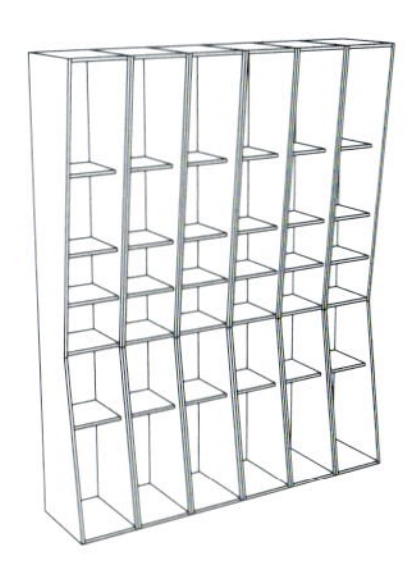

PADRE MARTINI

› Vedovamazzei
› Italy

This acid steel bookshelf was inspired by the painting of Padre Martini's bookshelf by Giuseppe Maria Crespi in ca. 1740. When loaded with books, the bookshelf becomes a painting.

XSHELF

› Hiromitsu Konishi / miso
› Japan

Xshelf is a flexible shelf designed with the theme of Japanese functional beauty, where simplicity and diversity coexist. Users can easily assemble the wood boards to have independent X forms. Coupling these X parts together allows users to use the shelf in different sizes and shapes. Easy de-installation and compactness make lower shipping cost and more convenient transportation possible. In addition, the X parts can be arranged vertically or horizontally to form a grid structure. The "X" refers to not only the shape of each part but also its multiple variations.

Photo ©Yuna Yagi

WABI SABI

I believe that the core of Japanese aesthetics could be defined by the word "Wabi Sabi", an expression for Japanese simplicity and sense of nature. "Wabi Sabi" values austerity and nature instead of decoration. For example, a Japanese product might not be much decorative but it offers "additional space" to feel the beauty of art and of life, as well as the "space" for more functions. Also, to design is to create space for users to perfect it and enjoy the process. That is the reason why products should be minimal while functional and versatile while long lasting. One of the main influences on my design, Japanese tea culture, also embodies "Wabi Sabi". The best definition of tea culture is "imperfection". The completion of design and production is not the end, in other words, it is not yet perfect. However, it is getting closer to perfection during the consumption.

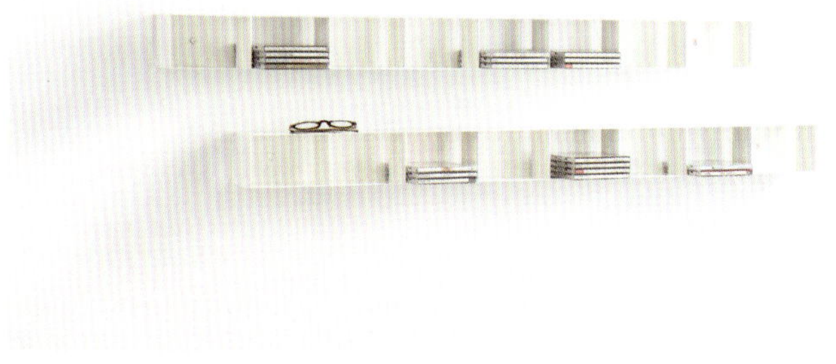

LUFT

» Anna Salonen
» Finland

Luft is an exceptional wall-shelf of timeless elegance. Being only 9cm wide, it can be placed almost anywhere. Because of its limited capacity for books, DVDs and CDs, the bookshelf does not completely disappear but remains partly visible. Luft can also be placed horizontally to achieve a stylish look.

EQUILIBRIUM

› Alejandro Gomez Stubbs
› Colombia

Equilibrium is a modular bookcase designed to break away from the traditional rigid and static look of bookshelves. With five modules stacked upon each other at angled points, the self-standing bookcase creates a surprising visual effect. Despite its floating effect, Equilibrium can hold up to 160 lbs of weight.

Usually books and magazines are not usually stored vertically. Common solutions to prevent them from sliding include bookends and decorative products. Equilibrium stores books in a natural tilted position without the need for bookends while maintaining an easy access. The piece can be disassembled for shipping. The modules can be nested inside each other and shipped in a single box that is easy to handle. It can be assembled in less than 5 minutes without any tools or hardware.

Photo ©Monica Barreneche

THE STORY BEHIND

The concepts behind Equilibrium are animation and surprise. I was inspired by things that make me happy: animated characters, trapeze acts and even some commercials. But I did not want to end up with a piece of furniture with eyes; I wanted to find animation in another context. I wanted to create a juxtaposition of the notion that books are heavy and static and the design to make it seem weightless. As if they were floating in the air.

Bringing Equilibrium from a concept to a commercial product was a real challenge. The first prototype was very inconvenient to transport and expensive to manufacture. We had to completely re-engineer the metal hardware that connected the modules and find a way to optimize functionality without compromising stability. The result was very gratifying. We came up with solution that allows the hardware to be discreetly hidden, while the whole product can be completely disassembled.

TREND

Historically the aesthetics of bookshelves has been driven by utilitarian purpose: to hold books or objects that are valuable, yet heavy and delicate. As the printed book is threatened by its digital counterpart, people began to see bookshelves more as a decorative item rather than as the shrine it used to be. This has led to the wider variety in bookshelf designs that have emerged in the last few years. From the perspective of a designer, this has allowed the modern bookshelves to become the focal point in the decor of a house for its style rather than its function. I would expect to see innovative bookshelves becoming more popular in the furniture.

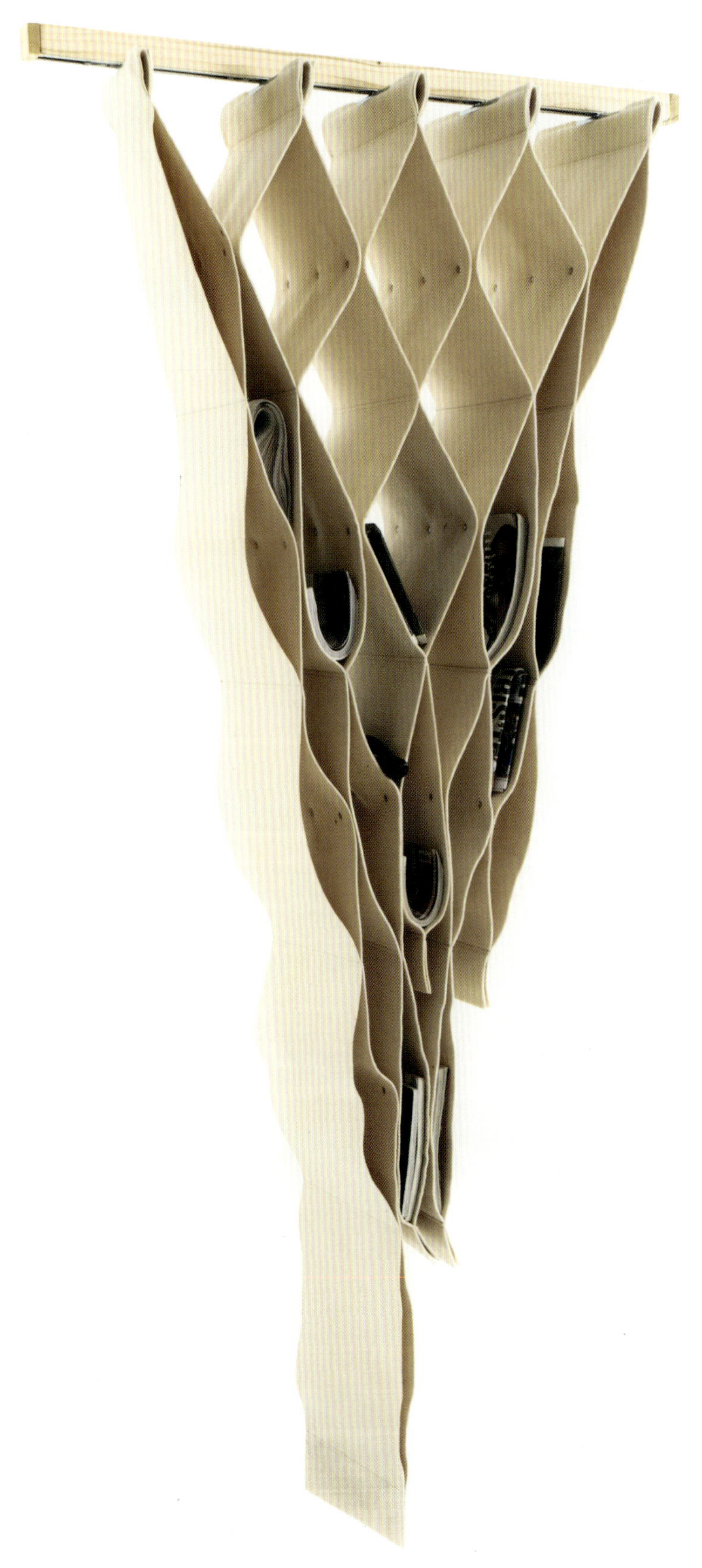

Photo ©Engin Yldız

BOOKWAVE

» Mehtap Obuz
» Turkey

Bookwave is a curtain, a room divider and a bookshelf. The soft nature of the fabric provides all these functions in a new approach as it expands to any size. This felt fabric storage unit with railing system was designed by Mehtap Obuz for ilio, the home product brand of Demirden Design.

THE STORY BEHIND

When I started to think of the bookshelf, the "form of energy" I had in mind was that reading books brings good energy. So I tried to focus on the flow of continuous soft lines and looked for what kind of material could express it, and it came out as the felt Bookwave. I thought of new offices or studios and decided that using a textile felt would make the atmosphere homely and warm, and also from a practical point of view, I wanted it to have two functions, a bookshelf as well as a room-divider curtain.

Photo ©Ezio Manciucca

ALL OVER

- Bruno Rainaldi
- Italy

The design philosophy for this project is that wall, packed with books and ornaments, needs shelves that make the most use of the available space. With this in mind, nothing is left empty and everything has its place. Open spaces and cabinets with doors create a fully functional composition.

SECTION SHELF

- Nathan Yong
- Italy

Section Shelf is a modular, self-standing bookcase in chalk-white lacquered metal. This project is a herringboned, diagonal system for optimizing spatial availability. Three modules with three different internal layouts satisfy various storage requirements for items such as books, magazines and office containers. The containers can be put together vertically or horizontally.

Photo ©Ezio Manciucca

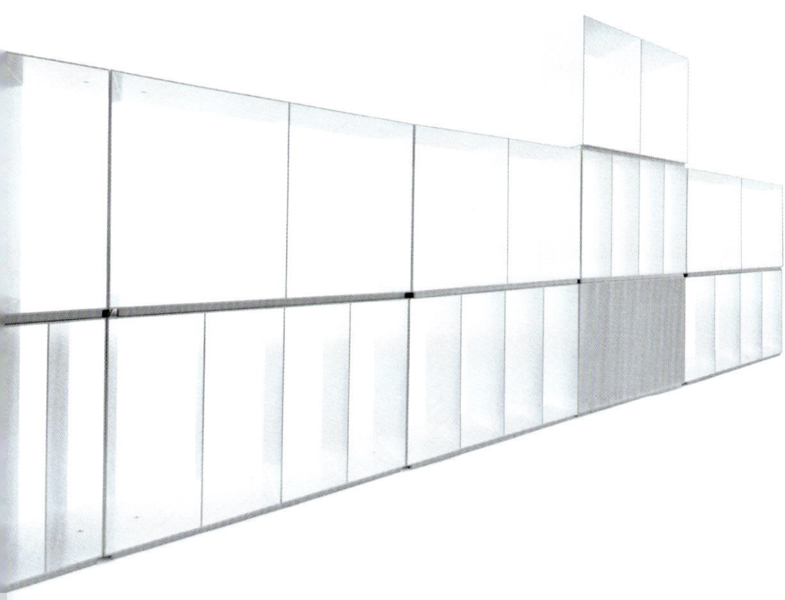

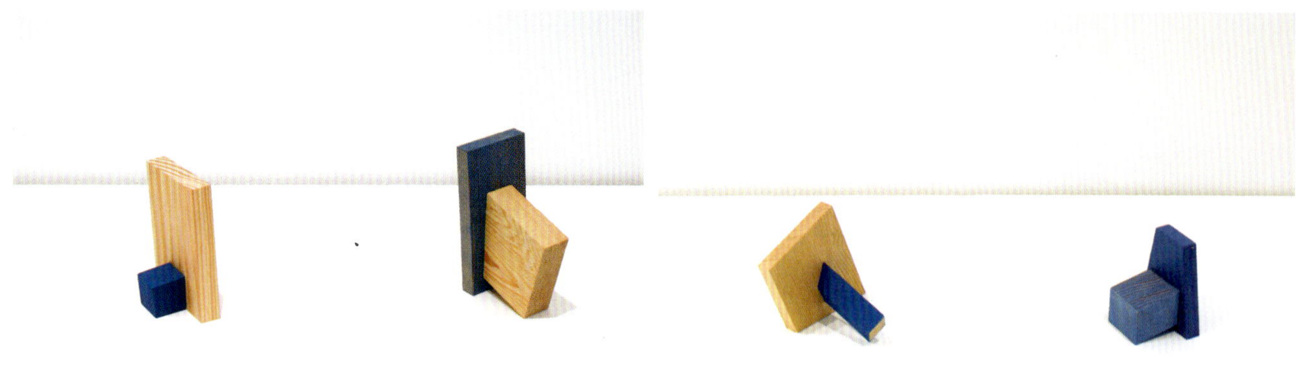

BOOK ENDS

› Amy Hunting
› UK

This project includes book supports with different structures and shades of blue. Irregular shapes of wood, left over after the "Felt and Gravity Collection" was made, together with blue pigment from an anamorphoscope were used to create these book ends.

Photo ©Oded Antman

THE FRAME-WORK

» Doron Andre Hadar / Labyrinth
» Spain

The Frame-work was created as a "bridge" connecting the designer and his late grandmother. It has a telescopic stainless steel cylinder that can change the distance between the wall and the frame. The position can be locked, depending on the depth of the books stored. The frame can be bent to improve the functionality, and let the book lay at an angle. The bookshelf product is handmade in different colors, sizes and styles.

CONTEMPLATE

» Yuri Shin
» Canada

This wall mounted bookshelf was designed to carry a message about environmental concerns that are closely tied to our daily activities. The bookshelf acts as a sign that warns and reminds the user about existing environmental issues like consumption rates as compared to the availability of raw material.

BEL.VEDERE

» Marcello Ziliani
» Italy

Books, but also plants and other items, give shape to the frame of a large mirror. Graphic symbols, colors, natural and artificial elements give this generous frame/container surrounding a mirror a lively and vibrant feel. It can be placed on the floor or hung on the wall, either vertically or horizontally.

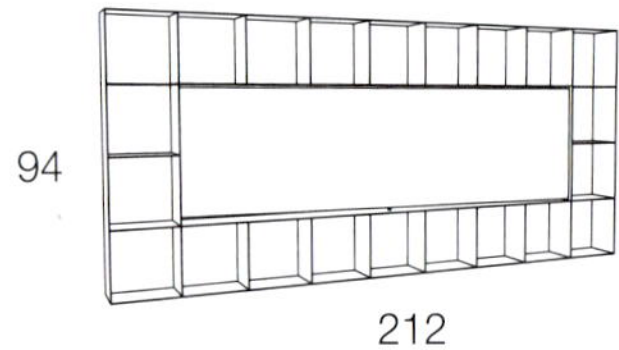

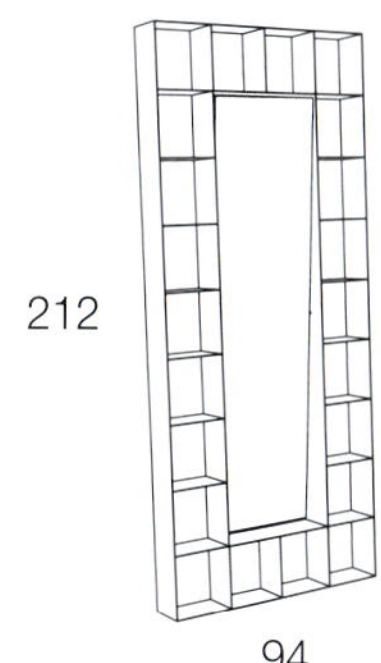

Photo ©Ezio Manciucca

Photo ©PH Vito Vippolis

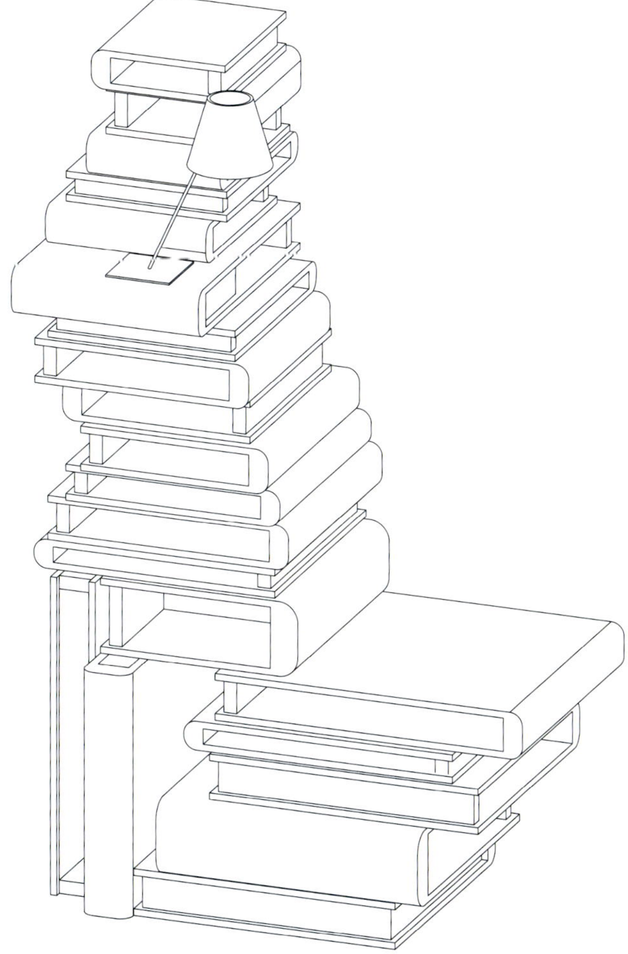

ONCE UPON A TIME

» Arch. Fabio Vinella
» Italy

The Once Upon a Time bookshelf is a walnut bookshelf, featuring a useful platform that can be a reading lamp, or made into a seat if you enjoy lounging amongst your favorite books. Each tome of the frame has a different size from the others.

THE STORY BEHIND & TREND

I used to sit on a pile of books while reading when I was a child. I enjoyed the intimacy of having books surrounding me, and I love the old tomes that covered my bedroom floor. Once Upon a Time came from these memories. When designing this bookshelf, I tried to find out the perfect balance between order and mess. It was designed to be innovative, evocative and in the meantime, comfortable. Comfort of readers matters a lot, and I think the future bookshelves will be more customer-oriented. Adaptability, for example, will be taken into consideration. Thus potentialities of dynamic frames will be explored for the customers to change the structure as they wish.

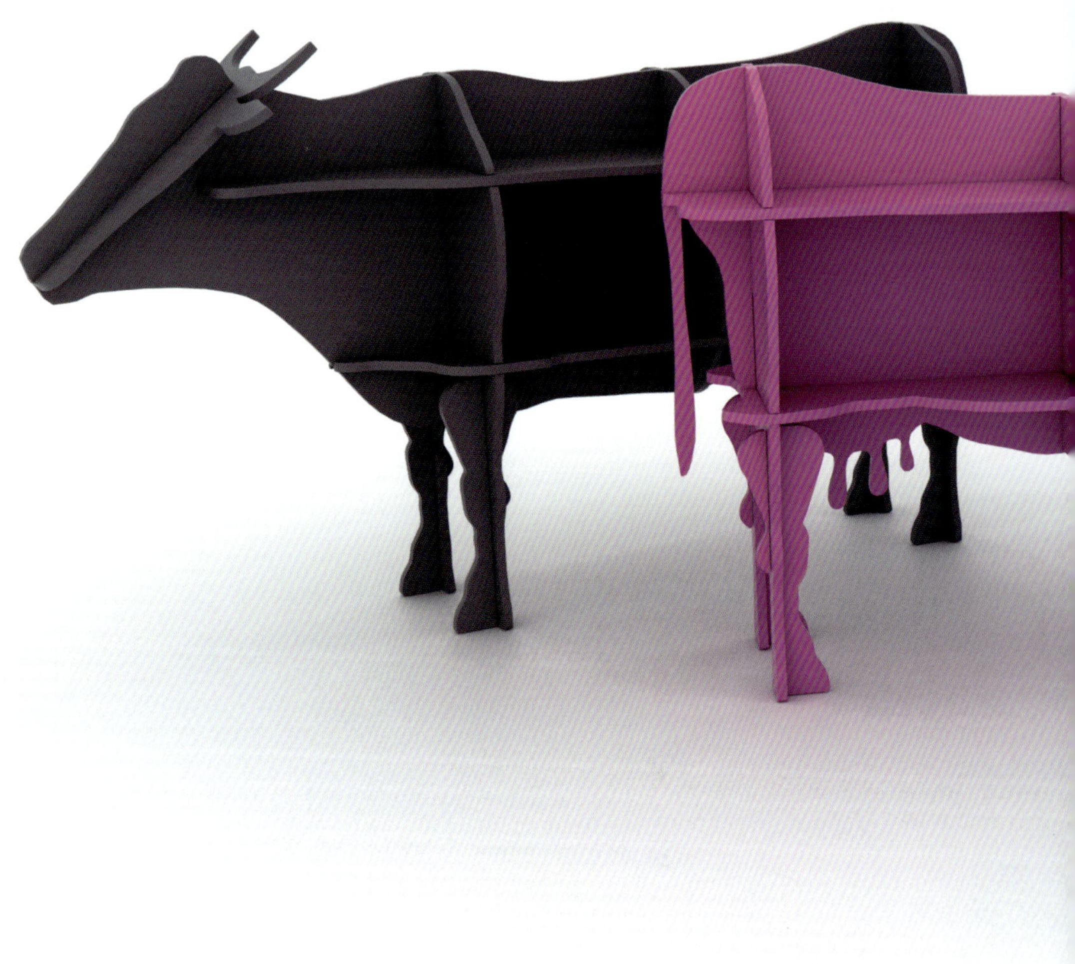

Photo ©Dennys

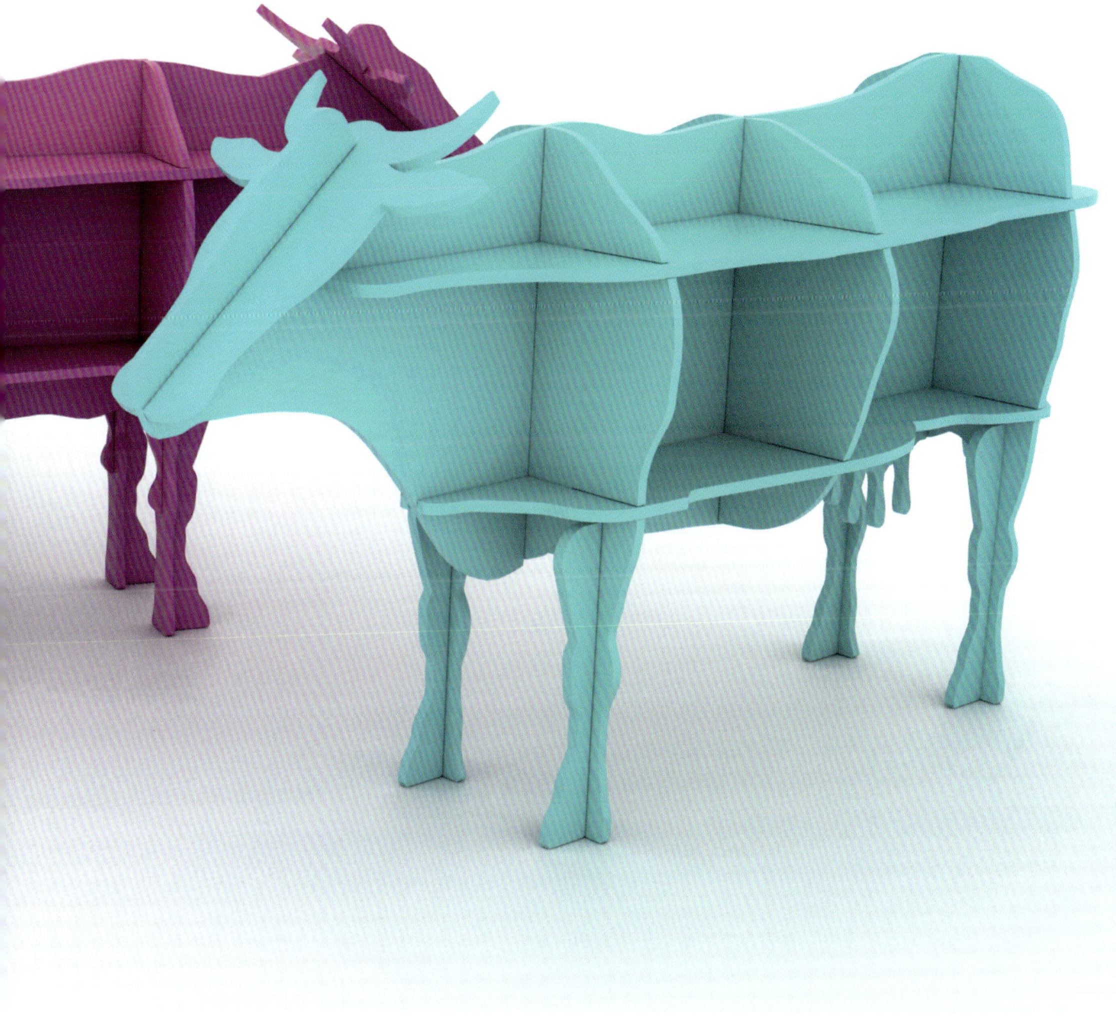

» Dennys Tormen, Glauco Bernardes
» Brazil

The Vaco bookshelf is exclusively assembled using pieces cut by a laser machine. The cow appearance is the most striking characteristics of this one of a kind design.

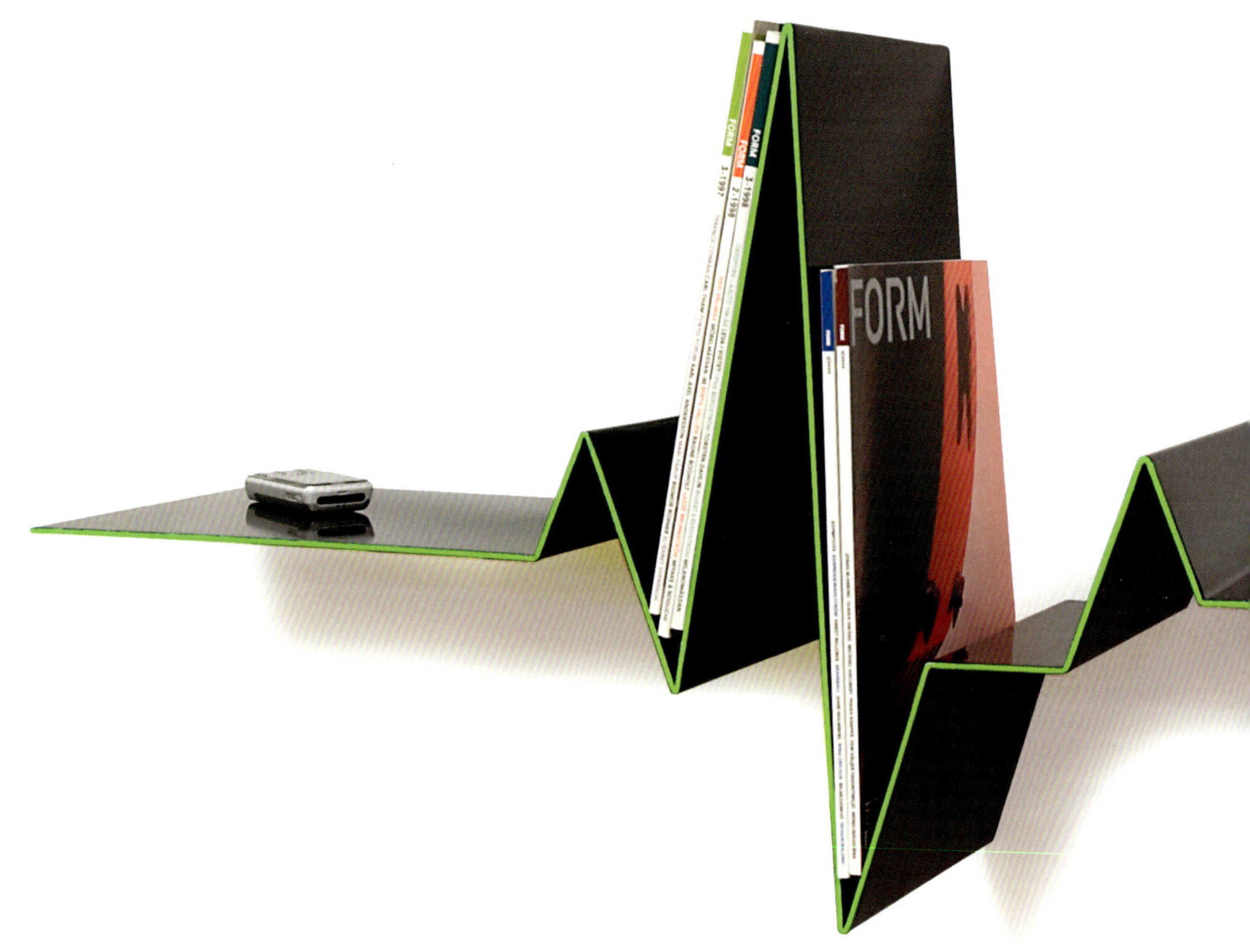

PULSELINE

» Måns Salomonsen
» Sweden

The designer simplified a heartbeat and glued some cardboard together to test what size was needed to hold some magazines and objects. The outline was painted green to enhance the look of heartbeat, so that people can recognize it from the cardiogram.

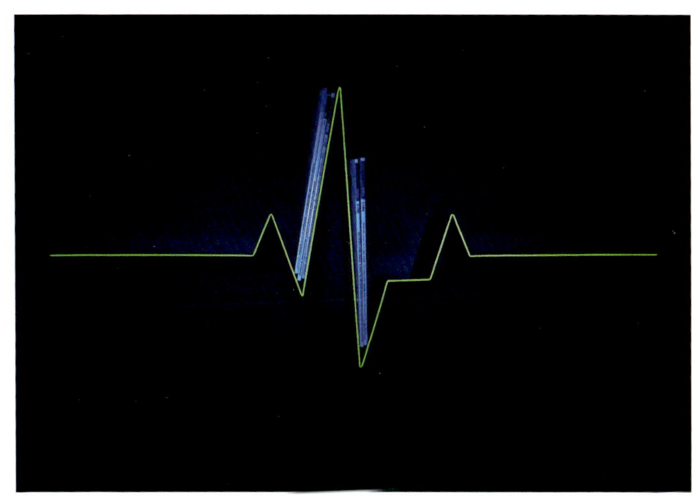

ON TREND

Bookshelves will be more and more decorative. The bookshelf today gains greater interior value than before. It has become a media that communicates style, function and new trends.

In many families, book collections are shrinking. And further changes can be seen since the development of electronic devices such as phones and pads. So in the future, books and magazines are more likely to be displayed than to be stored.

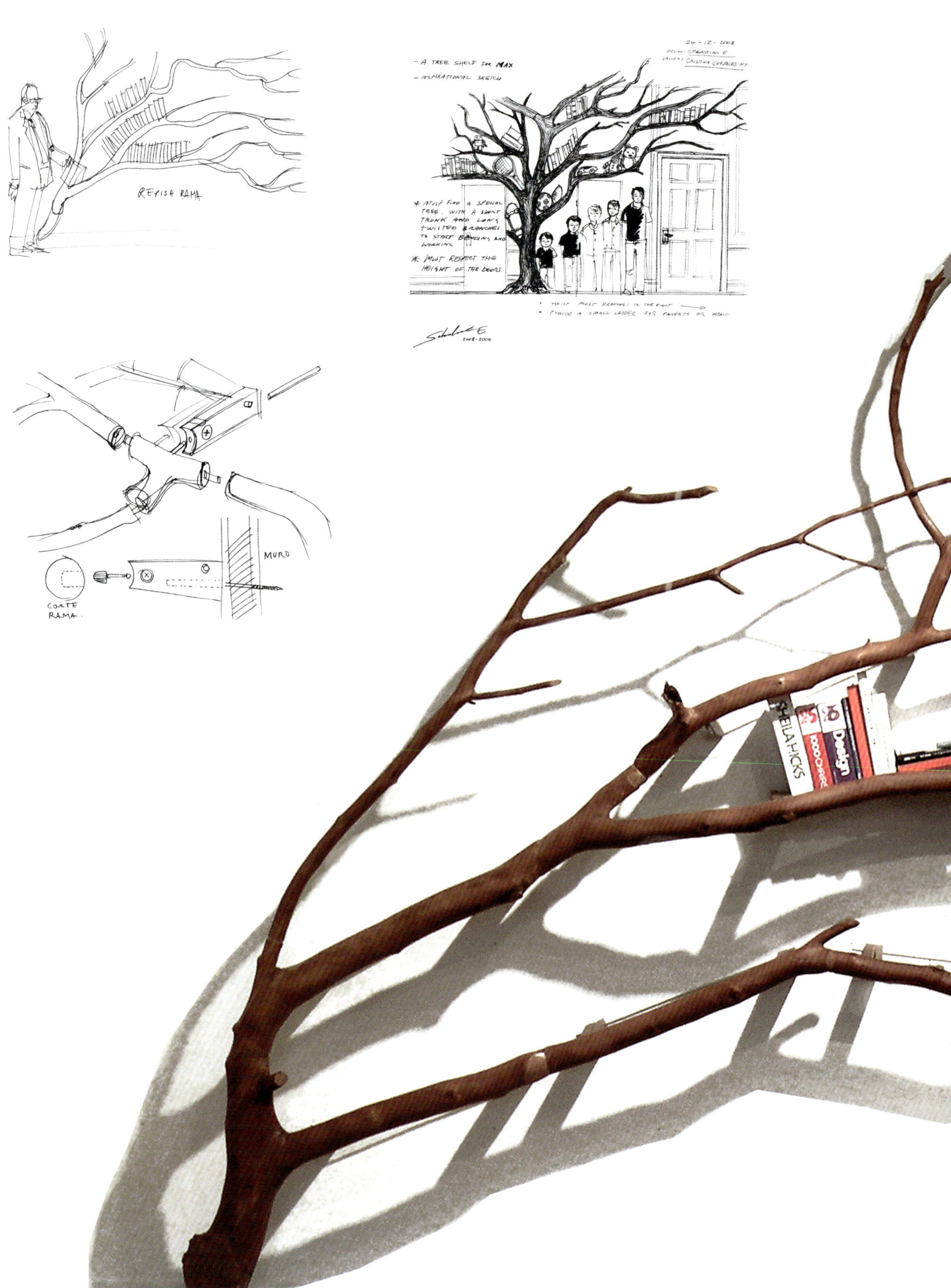
REPISA RAMA
24 - 12 - 2008
DESIGN: SEBASTIAN E
GALLERY: CRISTINA GRAJALES NY
- A TREE SHELF FOR MAX
- INSPIRATIONAL SKETCH
* MUST FIND A SPECIAL TREE, WITH A SHORT TRUNK AND LONG TWISTED BRANCHES TO START BENDING AND WORKING
* MUST RESPECT THE HEIGHT OF THE DOORS.
• TWIST MOST BRANCHES TO THE RIGHT
• PROVIDE A SMALL LADDER FOR PARENTS OR MAID
2008-2009
MURO
CORTE RAMA.
SHEILA HICKS
Design

BILBAO SHELF

» Sebastian Errazuriz
» Chile

The Bilbao Shelf got its name from the street in Santiago where the designer found this branch from a fallen tree. Then it was twisted, turned and readapted so it could lay flat against a wall as a bookshelf.

INDEX

Eva Paster, Michael Geldmacher
- www.neuland-id.de
- P058, P219

F.Cazzulo, S.Nunziato
- www.andviceversa.com
- P076

Fishtnk Design Factory
- www.fishtnk.com
- P028

Francesco Innocenti /Officina11 Studio
- www.officina11.it
- P190

Francesco Polare
- www.francescopolare.it
- P178

George Lee
- www.lemoutonnoirandco.com
- P172

Gerard de Hoop
- www.gerarddehoop.nl
- P082, P168, P169

Gian Marco Favretto
- www.behance.net/Gian_Design
- P200

Giovanni Gennari, Alisée Matta
www.nobodyandco.it
P027

Giulio Parini
- giulioparini.blogspot.com
- P093

Giuseppe Viganò
- giuseppevigano.it
- P184

Groupa Design studio
- www.groupastudio.com
- P012, P020

Gustav Johannsson, Agusta Magnusdottir /agustav
- www.agustav.com
- P160

Hans Tan
- hanstan.net
- P078

Helbert Suarez Ferreira, Remi Melander
- www.systemdesignstudio.com
- P236

Hideaki Asaoka
- www.behance.net/hideakiasaoka
P060

Hiromitsu Konishi /miso
- www.miso-miso.com
- P248

Hyunjin Seo
- kam-kam.org/studio
- P040

Ian Ortega
- www.pirwi.com
- P198

Isay Weinfeld
Landscape designer: Isabel Duprat
Graphic designer: Roberto Cipolla
www.isayweinfeld.com
P096

Jean & Oliver Pelle
- pelledesigns.com
- P130

Jiyoung Seo
- www.jiyoungseo.com
- P064

Joeri Reynaert
- www.joerireynaert.com
- P158

Jongho Park
- www.jonghopark.com
- P133

Jordi Pedemonte, Eric Castelló, Jon Azkoitia / Artik Project
- www.quattria.com/en/designers
- P202

Jorge Javier Cruz Florín
- www.behance.net/jorgejavier
- P196

Juil Kim
- www.designjoo.com
- P086

Jun Murakoshi
- junmurakoshi.com
- P014

Ka-Lai Chan
- www.kalaichan.nl
- P154

Kenyon Yeh
- www.kenyonyeh.com
- P126, P162, P224

Kylie Vickers
- www.kylie-vickers.co.uk
- P088

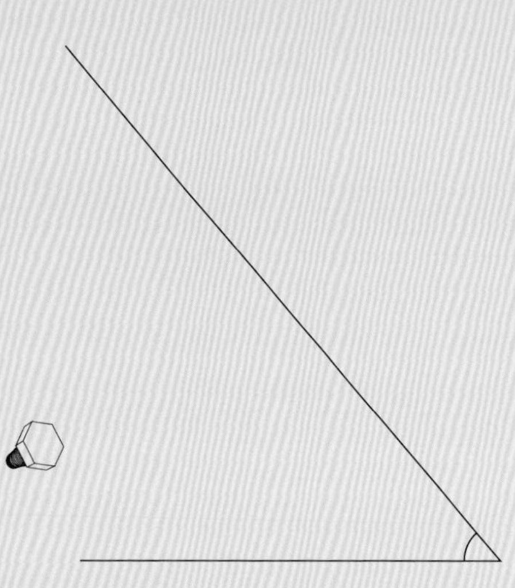

ACKNOWLEDGEMENTS

We would like to thank all the designers and contributers who have been involved in the production of this book. Their contribution is indispensable in the compilation of this book. We would also like to express our gratitude to all the producers for their invaluable opinions and assistance throughout this project. And to the many others whose names are not credited but have aided in the production of this book, we thank you for your continuous support.

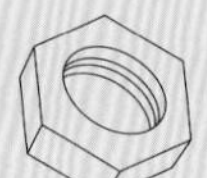

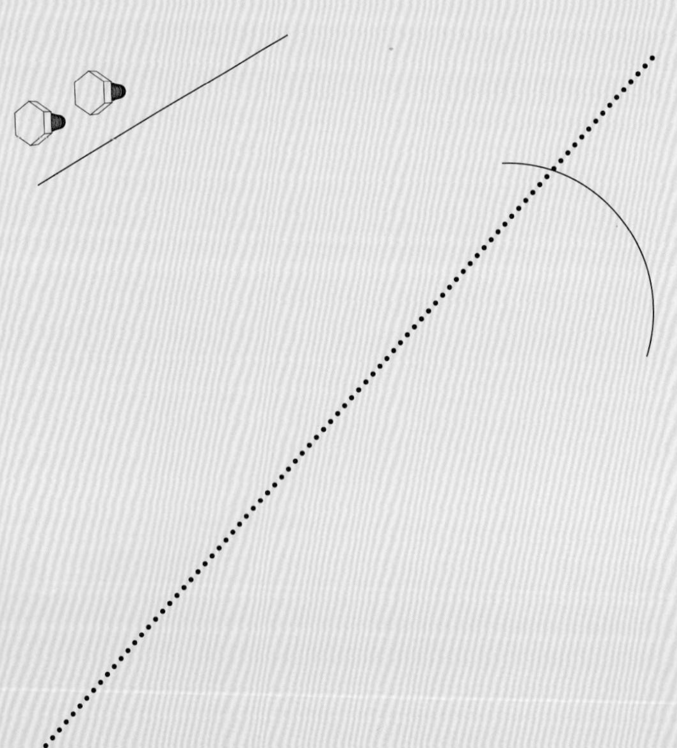

FUTURE COOPERATIONS: If you wish to participate in SendPoints' future projects and publications, please send your website or portfolio to editor01@sendpoints.cn